JULIA WALSH

2026

A Book of Grace-Filled Days

LoyolaPress.
A Jesuit Ministry

LOYOLA PRESS.
A JESUIT MINISTRY
www.loyolapress.com

Cover and interior design by Kathy Kikkert.

ISBN: 978-0-8294-5805-3

Published in Chicago, IL
Printed in Canada.
25 26 27 28 29 30 31 32 33 34 MQS 10 9 8 7 6 5 4 3 2 1

INTRODUCTION

With each new day, we are graced with a holy opportunity to unite with God.

This book is offered to support you in this mission of love.

As dawn illuminates landscapes, God gives us a fresh start. We inhale and exhale. We open our minds and hearts to God's guidance and love; we offer ourselves to service and contemplation. We say *yes* to the blessing and grace of morning.

As the sun moves overhead and warms the soil, air, and water, so too are we warmed by God's light. We may feel the need to surrender to God's love. Or, we may feel fear and grief. So we beckon Christ close and ask him to provide graces. We inhale and exhale. We awaken to nearby wonders: chirping birds and delicious food. We savor the sanctuaries: quiet chapels and kind souls. We say *yes* to the grace of a full day.

When the colors of dusk dance across the sky and the day's richness stirs through our minds, we are graced with a holy opportunity to reflect on our experience. Sometimes God's presence seems obvious: for this let us thank God. At other times, we acknowledge disappointment, danger, or division. Perhaps we regret our choices. Let us express our sorrow to God and pray for the mercy we need. We inhale, exhale, and invite calm into our bodies and minds. We say *yes* to the grace of a good night.

Sunday

NOVEMBER 30

• FIRST SUNDAY OF ADVENT •

They shall beat their swords into plowshares
and their spears into pruning hooks;
one nation shall not raise the sword against another,
nor shall they train for war again.
—ISAIAH 2:4

Today is the first Sunday of Advent, the start of a season of hope. For centuries, people have hoped for peace, justice, mercy, and freedom. Let's join our longings with theirs as we bring our Advent wreaths out of storage and make them centerpieces in our homes. Let's name our personal hopes and also pray for the hopes of the world. This is a good time to notice what occupies our hearts and minds. We can help prepare the world for the coming of Christ's peace by offering people comfort, solace, and life. By God's grace we are part of Christ's body: we are the peacemakers the world needs.

Isaiah 2:1–5
Psalm 122:1–2,3–4,4–5,6–7,8–9
Romans 13:11–14
Matthew 24:37–44

Monday

December 1

When Jesus entered Capernaum,
a centurion approached him and appealed to him.
—Matthew 8:5

When the centurion asked Jesus to tend to his servant, perhaps he felt doubtful that Jesus would help, or intimidated by Jesus and was afraid to ask. Certainly, the centurion felt care and concern. He offered Jesus his hopes, just as we can do. Maybe the centurion was surprised when Jesus responded with generosity and kindness. Maybe we feel surprised when God answers our prayers, too. No matter what we feel, we can count on Jesus's compassion.

Isaiah 4:2–6
Psalm 122:1–2,3–4b,4cd–5,6–7,8–9
Matthew 8:5–11

Tuesday

DECEMBER 2

He shall rescue the poor when he cries out.
—PSALM 72:12

Pope Francis has stated that, "Almost without being aware of it, we end up being incapable of feeling compassion at the outcry of the poor, weeping for other people's pain, and feeling a need to help them, as though all this were someone else's responsibility and not our own." When I encounter people in need, I try to have a compassionate heart, but sometimes I'm too distracted, busy, afraid, or inattentive. Yet I can't deny responsibility. I can offer food, coins, kindness, time, encouragement, and listening ears. If I get out of the way and allow God to use me, I may discover that, in rescuing others, I'm being rescued too.

Isaiah 11:1–10
Psalm 72:1–2,7–8,12–13,17
Luke 10:21–24

Wednesday

DECEMBER 3

• ST. FRANCIS XAVIER, PRIEST •

[Jesus said,] "I do not want to send them away hungry."
—MATTHEW 15:32

For a while, my parents owned a restaurant that was famous for its generous portions of food. Burgers weighed a whole pound. Having a steady supply of take-home containers was equally important as having ingredients and staff ready to feed the crowds. When checking people out at the cash register, my dad liked to chat with the guests who would usually say something like, "We're very full, but everything was delicious." My dad would smile and say, "Well, if anyone leaves here hungry, it might be their own fault." Jesus offers a feast to us at every Eucharistic liturgy. Better yet, the food is free.

Isaiah 25:6–10a
Psalm 23:1–3a,3b–4,5,6
Matthew 15:29–37

Thursday

DECEMBER 4

• ST. JOHN DAMASCENE, PRIEST AND DOCTOR OF THE CHURCH •

He humbles those in high places.
—ISAIAH 26:5

Love speaks to you: My beloved, you may like
to climb higher
and feel mighty and exalted. It may feel great to take in
the view from above.
But I need you on the ground, listening to the little ones.
I need you to see how mightily light shines through the faces
of the meek.
Come closer to me.

Isaiah 26:1–6
Psalm 118:1 and 8–9,19–21,25–27a
Matthew 7:21,24–27

Friday

DECEMBER 5

And their eyes were opened.
—MATTHEW 9:30

It's another day, and another opportunity to offer love to God, neighbor, and self. Do we see the chances to love nearby? Our vision may be clouded from exhaustion or stress. Are we trying to see everything according to our own ideas or agendas? Then perhaps we need to allow Christ to open our eyes.

Isaiah 29:17–24
Psalm 27:1,4,13–14
Matthew 9:27–31

Saturday

DECEMBER 6

• ST. NICHOLAS, BISHOP •

He heals the brokenhearted
and binds up their wounds.
He tells the number of the stars;
he calls each by name.
Great is our LORD and mighty in power:
to his wisdom there is no limit.
—PSALM 147:3–5

A man in my family once separated from us during a time of misunderstanding and stress. No one really knew what to do. We all prayed; we all felt brokenhearted. Then one day the man texted me and asked for a heart-to-heart. I said sure, and I listened, even though I was scared and sad. "I got my heart back," he said. It was a mystery to me what had happened, but I thanked God, who is powerful and wise.

Isaiah 30:19–21,23–26
Psalm 147:1–2,3–4,5–6
Matthew 9:35—10:1,5a,6–8

Sunday

DECEMBER 7

• SECOND SUNDAY OF ADVENT •

May the God of endurance and encouragement
grant you to think in harmony with one another,
in keeping with Christ Jesus,
that with one accord you may with one voice
glorify the God and Father of our Lord Jesus Christ.
—ROMANS 15:5–6

Musical harmony consists of a combination of notes and chords that don't clash but sound beautiful together. In our global church, we are a combination of personalities and cultures that can blend and create beauty. With God as the Great Conductor, we may need to get in tune and ensure there is room for the Spirit to flow through. Our diversity can be a gift. There can be harmony among us.

Come, Lord Jesus.

Isaiah 11:1–10
Psalm 72:1–2,7–8,12–13,17
Romans 15:4–9
Matthew 3:1–12

Monday

DECEMBER 8

• THE IMMACULATE CONCEPTION OF THE BLESSED VIRGIN MARY •

In him we were also chosen,
destined in accord with the purpose of the One
who accomplishes all things according to the
intention of his will
so that we might exist for the praise of his glory,
we who first hoped in Christ.
—EPHESIANS 1:11–12

Mary got to make a choice. God chose her to change the future. In the same way, each of us is chosen by God for particular purposes, and we each can choose to accept or reject God's plan for us. As we decide, Mary shows us that it's okay if we enter into conversation with the Holy One. We are permitted to ask questions, wonder, or feel troubled. We are graced to have Mary as our model and mother; the Blessed Mother who shows us how to be in a genuine relationship with God.

Genesis 3:9–15,20
Psalm 98:1,2–3ab,3cd–4
Ephesians 1:3–6,11–12
Luke 1:26–38

Tuesday

DECEMBER 9

• ST. JUAN DIEGO CUAUHTLATOATZIN, HERMIT •

Like a shepherd he feeds his flock;
in his arms he gathers the lambs,
Carrying them in his bosom,
and leading the ewes with care.
—ISAIAH 40:11

Sheep, like humans, are complex—they are both social *and* individualistic. They prefer to stay in their maternal family groups and follow a leader. They run when they're spooked but feel safer when they're with others. And sheep prefer to move toward light, not into darkness. It's definitely good news that our God is like a shepherd, then. We need a tender, wise guide to protect us, one who understands our behaviors and tendencies and who leads us with care.

Isaiah 40:1–11
Psalm 96:1–2,3 and 10ac,11–12,13
Matthew 18:12–14

Wednesday

DECEMBER 10

The LORD is the eternal God,
creator of the ends of the earth.
He does not faint nor grow weary,
and his knowledge is beyond scrutiny.
—ISAIAH 40:28

When labor and stress cause me to feel rundown, I'm comforted to know that God is close and involved in my life. When eyes droop and muscles ache, we can turn to the great Creator for comfort and strength. We may feel weary, but God does not tire of us or our needs.

Isaiah 40:25–31
Psalm 103:1–2,3–4,8 and 10
Matthew 11:28–30

Thursday

DECEMBER 11

• ST. DAMASUS I, POPE •

Your Kingdom is a Kingdom for all ages,
and your dominion endures through all generations.
—PSALM 145:13

Throughout human history, no monarch, prime minister, emperor, or president has been able to rule forever. No human leader has been able to have an impact on every generation, every person. We know that the God we adore has been ruling humanity since we started to roam the earth. And we await the coming of the true King, Jesus Christ—the only one who can claim us and rule over our hearts, minds, bodies, and behaviors. May we be ready to surrender to his might.

Isaiah 41:13–20
Psalm 145:1 and 9,10–11,12–13ab
Matthew 11:11–15

Friday

DECEMBER 12

• OUR LADY OF GUADALUPE •

You shall know that the LORD of hosts
has sent me to you.
—ZECHARIAH 2:15

Long ago on a hill named Tepeyac in what is now Mexico City, the mother of God appeared. Our Lady of Guadalupe didn't appear to the wealthy, proud, or powerful, but to a humble man named Juan Diego. Juan was sent by Our Lady to Bishop Zumárraga to share her message of love and hope. In this season of Advent, are we open to the messengers being sent to us? Let's get ready to receive and welcome others. Let's be open to making changes in response to the holy messengers God sends our way.

Zechariah 2:14–17 or Revelation 11:19a; 12:1–6a,10ab
Judith 13:18bcde,19
Luke 1:26–38 or 1:39–47

Saturday

DECEMBER 13

• ST. LUCY OF SYRACUSE, VIRGIN AND MARTYR •

Once again, O LORD of hosts,
look down from heaven, and see;
Take care of this vine,
and protect what your right hand has planted,
the son of man whom you yourself made strong.
—PSALM 80:15–16

Imagine a laborer wandering in his vineyard, inspecting his crops and taking note of what needs pruning and watering. He sees that there are insects and weeds to deal with. He begins to meditate on how he feels like a vine, connected to a lineage. He's aware he's growing and reaching forward in pursuit of the flourishing of God's will. The laborer prays with longing and hope that God will come and tend to his personhood, to prune away what's unnecessary so that he can remain strong for God's service. Now, imagine that your life is a vineyard. For what could you pray?

Sirach 48:1–4,9–11
Psalm 80:2ac and 3b,15–16,18–19
Matthew 17:9a,10–13

Sunday DECEMBER 14

• THIRD SUNDAY OF ADVENT •

You too must be patient.
Make your hearts firm,
because the coming of the Lord is at hand.
Do not complain, brothers and sisters, about one another,
that you may not be judged.
—JAMES 5:8–9

Human relationships are messy. God designed us to be social creatures with social needs: to belong, to be known, and to be needed. We each deserve to be loved. Yet we can be moody, mean, and self-centered. Despite our better intentions, we cause harm. When people hurt, confuse, and betray us, it's tough not to complain. There's one task we need not take on: judgment belongs to God.

Isaiah 35:1–6a,10
Psalm 146:6–7,8–9,9–10
James 5:7–10
Matthew 11:2–11

Monday

DECEMBER 15

So they said to Jesus in reply, "We do not know."
—MATTHEW 21:27

When the chief priests challenge Jesus and pepper him with questions, his response reveals who he is: gentle, provocative, and clever. As a wise teacher, he asks questions instead of giving answers. Jesus may also respond to our questions with questions. We may need to be ready to humbly admit our ignorance and say that we don't know the answer. We may need to accept the mysteries of faith.

Numbers 24:2–7,15–17a
Psalm 25:4–5ab,6 and 7bc,8–9
Matthew 21:23–27

Tuesday

DECEMBER 16

On that day
You need not be ashamed.
—ZEPHANIAH 3:11

In the spirit of the Advent season, let's consider what sort of hopes we're holding out to God. What are we waiting for? As we prepare for the arrival of the humble Christ born in a stable, we may need to let go of pride, selfishness, and shame. Let's ponder what needs to shift so that we can move toward joy and light.

Zephaniah 3:1–2,9–13
Psalm 34:2–3,6–7,17–18,19 and 23
Matthew 21:28–32

Wednesday

DECEMBER 17

He shall defend the afflicted among the people,
save the children of the poor.
—PSALM 72:4

As we open another flap on the Advent calendar, let's remember that counting down the days to Christmas is more than anticipating a delicious feast and fun gifts. Believing that Christ is both here *and* coming, and heaven is both now *and* not yet, we are also counting down to the time when every child living in poverty is free, when the oppressed are liberated, when the flourishing of God's peace and justice is widely known. We each have a part to play in this liberation, in the great countdown. Let's prepare for the arrival of an era when Christ's light fully burns out every form of oppression.

Genesis 49:2,8–10
Psalm 72:1–2,3–4ab,7–8,17
Matthew 1:1–17

Thursday

DECEMBER 18

The angel of the Lord appeared to him
in a dream and said,
"Joseph, son of David,
do not be afraid to take Mary your wife
into your home.
For it is through the Holy Spirit
that this child has been conceived in her."
—MATTHEW 1:20

Even if dreams don't become reality, they are already true and powerful. In our dreams, symbols and stories offer clues about deeper mysteries. Dreams can invite and direct our path. We may not be Joseph, but God speaks and communicates with us, too. Today, let's listen to our dreams and notice the guidance that God is offering.

Jeremiah 23:5–8
Psalm 72:1–2,12–13,18–19
Matthew 1:18–25

Friday

DECEMBER 19

And you will have joy and gladness,
and many will rejoice at his birth,
for he will be great in the sight of the Lord.
—LUKE 1:14–15

The Scripture readings today are about the conception of two different sons: Samson, and John the Baptist. In both cases, their mothers conceived when they were thought to be beyond their childbearing years. As parents-to-be, the women were expected to abstain from alcohol. The boys were filled with the Spirit and revealed God's might. Let us also be open to new life and wonder. We may need to abstain from something so as to prepare for an arrival. Little is required as we anticipate the miracle of birth—of God choosing to humbly take on human nature and dwell among us. Let's get ready to sing "Joy to the World."

Judges 13:2–7,24–25a
Psalm 71:3–4a,5–6ab,16–17
Luke 1:5–25

Saturday

DECEMBER 20

Then the angel said to her,
"Do not be afraid, Mary,
for you have found favor with God."
—LUKE 1:30

It seems that the angel's acknowledgment of Mary's fear somehow gave Mary the courage to say *yes*. When we hear "Don't be afraid," we feel seen and encouraged. It's as if our fear needs to be named and known for it to lose its power. Maybe we can be like angels for one another: We can name and notice what others are suffering from and validate their fears. We can encourage one another to receive God's grace. Everyone needs support.

Isaiah 7:10–14
Psalm 24:1–2,3–4ab,5–6
Luke 1:26–38

Sunday

DECEMBER 21

• FOURTH SUNDAY OF ADVENT •

Therefore the Lord himself will give you this sign:
the virgin shall conceive, and bear a son,
and shall name him Emmanuel.
—ISAIAH 7:14

Today, we light the fourth candle on our Advent wreath,
knowing that the day of the Lord is near.
And, we know that Jesus is Emmanuel, God with us.
When we feel the pangs of new life forming,
pregnancy or otherwise, God with us.
When we are too tired and in pain, God with us.
When there's no way to pay the bills, God with us.
When people are hungry and oppressed, God with us.
When violence feels stronger than love, God with us.
When despair comes easier than hope, God with us.
When we need to trust that we are held through it all,
God with us.

Isaiah 7:10–14
Psalm 24:1–2,3–4,5–6 (7c and 10b)
Romans 1:1–7
Matthew 1:18–24

Monday

DECEMBER 22

[Hannah said,] "I prayed for this child, and the LORD granted my request.
Now I, in turn, give him to the LORD;
as long as he lives, he shall be dedicated to the LORD."
—1 SAMUEL 1:27–28

I asked my friend what inspired him to enter religious life. He told me how he had a life-threatening illness, faced his mortality, and asked for God to save his life. When his illness went away, he desired to give his life back to God. Because he was grateful, he wanted to dedicate himself to God and worship God for the rest of his life. This is a modern story I am telling you, and it is also the story of salvation history, of the lives of the saints. Because of gratitude, each of us can dedicate our lives to God.

1 Samuel 1:24–28
1 Samuel 2:1,4–5,6–7,8abcd
Luke 1:46–56

Tuesday

DECEMBER 23

• ST. JOHN OF KANTY, PRIEST •

All the paths of the LORD are kindness and constancy
toward those who keep his covenant and his decrees.
—PSALM 25:10

Faced with big and small decisions, we can become overwhelmed by indecisiveness. We grip maps and tune in to the GPS, hoping to know the right way to go. What will line up with God's will? What choices must we make so that the future is full of God's goodness? It turns out the pathway that God has provided is lined with mercy. Pit stops and road signs profess truth. Let's turn away from selfishness, fear, and lies. Let's make our destinations mercy and truth.

Malachi 3:1–4,23–24
Psalm 25:4–5ab,8–9,10 and 14
Luke 1:57–66

Wednesday

DECEMBER 24

"You, my child, shall be called the prophet
of the Most High,
for you will go before the Lord to prepare his way,
to give his people knowledge of salvation
by the forgiveness of their sins.
In the tender compassion of our God
the dawn from on high shall break upon us,
to shine on those who dwell in darkness
and the shadow of death,
and to guide our feet into the way of peace."
—LUKE 1:76–79

Much of what John the Baptist was called to do remains relevant in our time. By our attitudes and actions, we, too, can give people knowledge of salvation and reveal God's mercy. Our cooperation with the Spirit can allow others to see God's light. We can each walk the path of peace. With God's grace, we can take the first step.

2 Samuel 7:1–5,8b–12,14a,16
Psalm 89:2–3,4–5,27 and 29
Luke 1:67–79

Thursday

DECEMBER 25

• THE NATIVITY OF THE LORD (CHRISTMAS) •

They shall name him Emmanuel,
which means "God is with us."
—MATTHEW 1:23

Because Jesus was born, and God humbled himself, became human, and dwelt among us, everything changed. Because of how God arrived—in a simple stable—we know where to look for God. The Jesuit mystic Pierre Teilhard de Chardin wrote, "By virtue of Creation, and still more the Incarnation, nothing here below is profane for those who know how to see." God is here. God is near. All is holy. Love is present, changing everything. Let's see God's love today and celebrate with joy. Merry Christmas!

VIGIL:
Isaiah 62:1–5
Psalm 89:4–5,16–17,27,29 (2a)
Acts 13:16–17,22–25
Matthew 1:1–25

NIGHT:
Isaiah 9:1–6
Psalm 96:1–2,2–3,11–12,13
Titus 2:11–14
Luke 2:1–14

DAWN:
Isaiah 62:11–12
Psalm 97:1,6,11–12
Titus 3:4–7
Luke 2:15–20

DAY:
Isaiah 52:7–10
Psalm 98:1,2–3,3–4,5–6 (3c)
Hebrews 1:1–6
John 1:1–18

Friday

DECEMBER 26

• ST. STEPHEN, THE FIRST MARTYR •

Stephen, filled with grace and power,
was working great wonders and signs
among the people.
—ACTS 6:8

There are people in our faith communities who, like Stephen, are filled with grace and power and work great wonders and signs among us. They could be labeled a threat to the status quo; perhaps we don't like them or what they are saying. We are disturbed and begin to resist. We may become cruel and suck the goodness—and life—out of them. Let us not make the holy ones in our midst into martyrs by our disrespect. Let's be open to the positive forces for good in our midst. Let's protect the lives and the power of these people.

Acts 6:8–10; 7:54–59
Psalm 31:3cd–4,6 and 8ab,16bc and 17
Matthew 10:17–22

Saturday

DECEMBER 27

• ST. JOHN, APOSTLE AND EVANGELIST •

For the life was made visible;
we have seen it and testify to it
and proclaim to you the eternal life
that was with the Father and was made visible to us—
what we have seen and heard
we proclaim now to you.
—1 JOHN 1:2–3

In the ordinary and unusual, we can see the power of God: in light shining, breezes blowing, hearty handshakes, or nourishing food. In every direction and in each moment, it is revealed to us that Life—Christ—is close. Not everyone can easily see the glory and the goodness, however. If you are one who can see the Life that is visible, an invitation is offered: testify and proclaim, and by doing so, help others notice Life too.

1 John 1:1–4
Psalm 97:1–2,5–6,11–12
John 20:1a and 2–8

Sunday

DECEMBER 28

• THE HOLY FAMILY OF JESUS, MARY, AND JOSEPH •

And let the peace of Christ control your hearts,
the peace into which you were also called in one body.
And be thankful.
—COLOSSIANS 3:15

Family life can be vibrant and formative, full of celebrations, traditions, love, affirmation, and food. We gain an understanding of ourselves, our faith, and our gifts when we are among those who love us. Yet no family is spared from misunderstandings, hurt, and sorrow. It can be good news to know that Jesus, Mary, and Joseph may have dealt with similar struggles. Even with all the ups and downs, we can be grateful.

Sirach 3:2–6,12–14
Psalm 128:1–2,3,4–5
Colossians 3:12–21
Matthew 2:13–15,19–23

Monday

DECEMBER 29

• ST. THOMAS BECKET, BISHOP AND MARTYR •

Whoever says, "I know him," but does not keep his commandments is a liar, and the truth is not in him.

—1 JOHN 2:4

It's tough to tend to our interior life *and* be present to others. There's a need for balancing what we experience in our bodies, minds, and souls with honoring the complexities of community life. When we maintain good balance in all aspects of life, it's easier to authentically be ourselves with others. When we're off balance, though, we may become inconsistent, untrue to ourselves and others as a result of tension and inner conflicts. By God's grace, we can be true to God, each other, and ourselves.

1 John 2:3–11
Psalm 96:1–2a,2b–3,5b–6
Luke 2:22–35

Tuesday

DECEMBER 30

He governs the peoples with equity.
—PSALM 96:10

As a child, I knew the meaning of something being "fair" long before I was familiar with the word *justice*. If one of my siblings was favored more than I or my cousin got a bigger cookie from my grandma, I whined that the situation was "not fair!" As adults we may talk to God the same way, complaining about how we try to do the right thing but everything is too complicated. We each could prayerfully consider how our trust in God's fairness and justice deepens as we grow up.

1 John 2:12–17
Psalm 96:7–8a,8b–9,10
Luke 2:36–40

Wednesday

DECEMBER 31

• ST. SYLVESTER I, POPE •

In the beginning was the Word,
and the Word was with God,
and the Word was God.
—JOHN 1:1

Consider how much God and words have in common. Both God and words build the bonds of relationship. Like God, words connect, inform, inspire, and provide. Just as words weave us together and make us new, so, too, does God. God, who is the Word, is here now, thanks to the birth of Christ. For all of this, we can pray: *O God, help me to revere the holy power of the Word. Amen.*

1 John 2:18–21
Psalm 96:1–2,11–12,13
John 1:1–18

Thursday

JANUARY 1

• THE SOLEMNITY OF MARY, THE HOLY MOTHER OF GOD •

*When the fullness of time had come, God sent his Son,
born of a woman.*
—GALATIANS 4:4

On New Year's Eve, my Franciscan community gathers in the chapel for a special ritual to bless time. We hold up our calendars and clocks and pray for God to be with us in each minute, hour, and day. Today, on New Year's Day—and indeed on every day—let us pause to consider how God can bless and guide us through the sacredness of time. As God's fullness was revealed through Mary, so too can God's fullness be revealed through us every minute of our lives.

Numbers 6:22–27
Psalm 67:2–3,5,6,8 (2a)
Galatians 4:4–7
Luke 2:16–21

Friday

JANUARY 2

• ST. BASIL THE GREAT AND ST. GREGORY NAZIANZEN,
BISHOPS AND DOCTORS OF THE CHURCH •

And now, children, remain in him,
so that when he appears we may have confidence
and not be put to shame by him at his coming.
—1 JOHN 2:28

How do we know we are remaining in Christ? Maybe we don't know it in our minds but we do know it in our bodies: as our hands cook food for the hungry, as we bow in reverence, as we kneel in prayer, as we hold someone who needs comfort. Maybe we show that we belong to God through our behavior.

1 John 2:22–28
Psalm 98:1,2–3ab,3cd–4
John 1:19–28

Saturday JANUARY 3

• THE MOST HOLY NAME OF JESUS •

Sing joyfully to the LORD, all you lands;
break into song; sing praise.
—PSALM 98:4

Have you ever walked across a prairie, along a desert trail, or deep in the woods and realized you were surrounded by a symphony? The earth and all its elements model for us how to give praise to God. We can follow the example of the wind, birds, and fluttering leaves and lift our voices to God in praise. Let's join the joyful harmony of creation.

1 John 2:29—3:6
Psalm 98:1,3cd–4,5–6
John 1:29–34

Sunday

January 4

• THE EPIPHANY OF THE LORD •

Raise your eyes and look about;
they all gather and come to you:
your sons come from afar,
and your daughters in the arms of their nurses.

Then you shall be radiant at what you see,
your heart shall throb and overflow,
for the riches of the sea shall be emptied out before you,
the wealth of nations shall be brought to you.
—Isaiah 60:4–5

God's majesty is expansive and beautiful. No matter our circumstances, we can join the nations and adore God's beauty. One way to do this is to generously share our wealth and make room for others. We can be like Mary and Joseph and welcome guests. May we be like the Holy Family, open and receptive to all.

Isaiah 60:1–6
Psalm 72:1–2,7–8,10–11,12–13
Ephesians 3:2–3a,5–6
Matthew 2:1–12

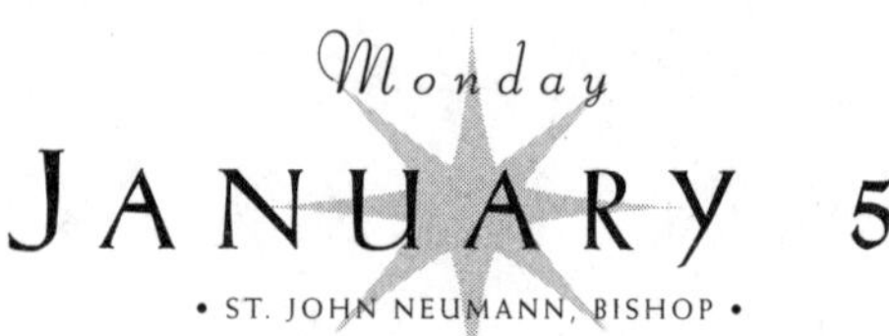

Monday

JANUARY 5

• ST. JOHN NEUMANN, BISHOP •

Love one another just as he commanded us.
—1 JOHN 3:23

St. Francis of Assisi is known for saying, "Preach the gospel at all times; when necessary, use words." Our gestures communicate more than our speech. We can talk about being available for others, but unless we show up for them in the good as well as the tough moments of their lives and offer loving presence, then, well, we are just saying we have good intentions. Today, let's choose to show our love through acts of kindness.

1 John 3:22—4:6
Psalm 2:7bc–8,10–12a
Matthew 4:12–17,23–25

Tuesday

JANUARY 6

• ST. ANDRÉ BESSETTE, RELIGIOUS •

Then, taking the five loaves and the two fish
and looking up to heaven,
he said the blessing, broke the loaves,
and gave them to his disciples
to set before the people;
he also divided the two fish among them all.
They all ate and were satisfied.
And they picked up twelve wicker baskets
full of fragments
and what was left of the fish.
—MARK 6:41–43

Jesus shows us how to live in a spirit of abundance. He invited people to sit together, and he made an offering of himself and of food, energy, time, and prayer. He blessed and became a blessing. He provided for the hungry. No one was left out. Everyone had more than enough. In fact, there were leftovers. May we live in a spirit of abundance, too.

1 John 4:7–10
Psalm 72:1–2,3–4,7–8
Mark 6:34–44

Wednesday

JANUARY 7

• ST. RAYMOND OF PEÑAFORT, PRIEST •

No one has ever seen God.
Yet, if we love one another, God remains in us,
and his love is brought to perfection in us.
—1 JOHN 4:12

It's easy to read the Scriptures and overthink. We might be tempted to make the word of God into a riddle to be solved, pondering, "What am I missing?" But then a whisper comes: *To know who God is, look for love.* "But—" we might protest. Again, the whisper: *To see God, love. To be united with God, love.* So let's stop talking and listen. Let's learn from him how to love.

1 John 4:11–18
Psalm 72:1–2,10,12–13
Mark 6:45–52

Thursday

JANUARY 8

"The Spirit of the Lord is upon me,
because he has anointed me
to bring glad tidings to the poor.
He has sent me to proclaim liberty to captives
and recovery of sight to the blind,
to let the oppressed go free,
and to proclaim a year acceptable to the Lord."
—LUKE 4:18–19

Jesus offers freedom. When it's tough to see what's real, when a person is stubborn or clueless, when oppressive ways cause people to be stuck, when anyone causes harm to others or to oneself, Jesus is ready to liberate. When selfishness, pride, or greed get in the way of mercy, joy, and hope, Jesus enters in. Jesus changes everything.

1 John 4:19—5:4
Psalm 72:1–2,14 and 15bc,17
Luke 4:14–22

Friday

JANUARY 9

The Spirit is truth.
—1 JOHN 5:6

With so much information coming at us every day, we may have good reasons to doubt and distrust. Fortunately, we can trust that God will reveal what is true; God is truth. Let's invite God to help us know the truth.

1 John 5:5–13
Psalm 147:12–13,14–15,19–20
Luke 5:12–16

Saturday

JANUARY 10

[John said,] "He must increase; I must decrease."
—JOHN 3:30

John the Baptist gives a formula for getting out of God's way so that Christ can shine bright: More Jesus, less pride. More mercy, less selfishness. More compassion, less ego. More love, less fear.

More we, less me.
By your grace, Good God,
may it be. Amen.

1 John 5:14–21
Psalm 149:1–2,3–4,5 and 6a and 9b
John 3:22–30

Sunday

JANUARY 11

• THE BAPTISM OF THE LORD •

After Jesus was baptized,
he came up from the water and behold,
the heavens were opened for him,
and he saw the Spirit of God descending like a dove
and coming upon him.
And a voice came from the heavens, saying,
"This is my beloved Son, with whom I am
well pleased."
—MATTHEW 3:16–17

There's so much action in this story! Jesus came up from the water. The heavens opened. The Spirit of God descended. A voice was heard. All these years later, God remains with us, full of action. God is still speaking: compassionate messages ring out through Scripture, tradition, people, and creation. Listen closely; you may be invited into the action.

Isaiah 42:1–4,6–7
Psalm 29:1–2,3–4,3,9–10 (11b)
Acts 10:34–38
Matthew 3:13–17

Monday

JANUARY 12

[Jesus said,] "This is the time of fulfillment.
The Kingdom of God is at hand.
Repent, and believe in the Gospel."
—MARK 1:15

Jesus proclaimed these words at the start of his public ministry, and he proclaims them to us today. The time of fulfillment is still unfolding, and the peace and justice that Christ established are here. The Kingdom of God is close at hand. Let's show that we believe the Good News.

1 Samuel 1:1–8
Psalm 116:12–13,14–17,18–19
Mark 1:14–20

Tuesday

JANUARY 13

• ST. HILARY, BISHOP AND DOCTOR OF THE CHURCH •

The people were astonished at his teaching,
for he taught them as one having authority
and not as the scribes.
—MARK 1:22

To be astonished means to be surprised and impressed. Every day, Jesus is pouring out grace and mercy to us, and the Spirit is teaching us truth. Yet we can still experience the doldrums of the mundane. How can our hearts and minds be open to God's beauty and love that are present in what's ordinary? The dishes to be washed, the e-mails to be read, the bed to be made? The ordinary is sacred and ought to astonish. Today, let's pray for the grace to feel astonishment for God's love.

1 Samuel 1:9–20
1 Samuel 2:1,4–5,6–7,8abcd
Mark 1:21–28

Wednesday

JANUARY 14

The LORD came and revealed his presence,
calling out as before: "Samuel, Samuel!"
Samuel answered, "Speak, for your servant is listening."
—1 SAMUEL 3:10

When I was a child, alone in my dark bedroom, I would squeeze my eyes tight and strain to hear God's voice in the quiet, hoping that God would make his will clear to me as he did for Samuel. Each of us can offer God our listening hearts and our willingness. We are called to respond to God's might, to surrender and trust. Let us listen to God's invitation to serve today.

1 Samuel 3:1–10,19–20
Psalm 40:2 and 5,7–8a,8b–9,10
Mark 1:29–39

Thursday

JANUARY 15

A leper came to him and kneeling down
begged him and said,
"If you wish, you can make me clean."
Moved with pity, he stretched out his hand,
touched the leper, and said to him,
"I do will it. Be made clean."
—MARK 1:40–41

The leper believed in Jesus's healing power. He reverenced Jesus and invited him to transform his suffering. And he was open to Jesus's will: "If you wish," the leper said. We deal with suffering in our lives too. In and with Christ, we each have the power to be instruments of healing and transformation. Christ's healing provides belonging. Today, let us reach out and include someone in community.

1 Samuel 4:1–11
Psalm 44:10–11,14–15,24–25
Mark 1:40–45

Friday

JANUARY 16

Unable to get near Jesus because of the crowd,
they opened up the roof above him.
After they had broken through,
they let down the mat on which the paralytic
was lying.
—MARK 2:4

Imagine it: There are so many people crammed into the house that you and your friends are unsure how to introduce your buddy—the paralytic on a mat—to Jesus. What can you do? Someone in the circle suggests going down through the roof. You think it's a ridiculous idea, but you go along, lifting up your friend. You help open the roof and lower your friend into the house. How does the crowd react when there's all the commotion? Are some people laughing? Are others annoyed or angry? Notice Jesus's compassion. Let's imitate that compassion today, despite chaotic interruptions.

1 Samuel 8:4–7,10–22a
Psalm 89:16–17,18–19
Mark 2:1–12

Saturday

JANUARY 17

• ST. ANTHONY, ABBOT •

[Jesus said,] "Those who are well do not need a physician,
but the sick do.
I did not come to call the righteous but sinners."
—MARK 2:17

By his humility, Jesus turned the expected order upside down. Jesus was present to the lowly, to sinners, and to those in need of healing. He was sovereign and mighty but preferred people who felt they had little power or influence—the weak and the ill, people like us. *Jesus, be present, and influence me today as I share your presence with others. Amen.*

1 Samuel 9:1–4,17–19; 10:1
Psalm 21:2–3,4–5,6–7
Mark 2:13–17

Sunday

JANUARY 18

• SECOND SUNDAY IN ORDINARY TIME •

I have waited, waited for the LORD,
and he stooped toward me and heard my cry.
—PSALM 40:1–2

The maker of the entire universe is not too distant for any of our cries or troubles. Through the wonder of Jesus's life, Death, and Resurrection, there is no place in the human experience that is too low for God. We may feel as if we're waiting in the muck for too long, but God is with us in all that we're dealing with, ready to hold us in our heartache. God hears us. God is love.

Isaiah 49:3,5–6
Psalm 40:2,4,7–8,8–9,10 (8a,9a)
1 Corinthians 1:1–3
John 1:29–34

Monday

JANUARY 19

[Jesus said,] "No one sews a piece of unshrunken cloth
on an old cloak.
If he does, its fullness pulls away,
the new from the old, and the tear gets worse.
Likewise, no one pours new wine into old wineskins.
Otherwise, the wine will burst the skins,
and both the wine and the skins are ruined.
Rather, new wine is poured into fresh wineskins."
—MARK 2:21–22

Jesus understood the human inclination to stay stuck in old ways, in what's comfortable and predictable. But the gospel way—the way of Christ—upsets the status quo. Each step we take with Jesus on the path of love is a step into deeper transformation. Our old patterns and structures won't work when we're making a fresh start. Are we open to the new wine and fresh wineskins that are being offered?

1 Samuel 15:16–23
Psalm 50:8–9,16bc–17,21 and 23
Mark 2:18–22

Tuesday

JANUARY 20

• ST. FABIAN, POPE AND MARTYR * ST. SEBASTIAN, MARTYR •

Then he said to them,
"The sabbath was made for man, not man
for the sabbath."
—MARK 2:27

Since the Industrial Revolution, the Catholic Church has expressed its concern about people being treated more like machines than like children of God. The church objects to unsafe working conditions, low pay, and long hours. Our dignity—our value and worth—is determined not by what we produce but by our very being. And God loves us so much that God established a commandment that we take a Sabbath; that one-seventh of our time is centered on restoration, rest, and recreation. When our bodies and minds are renewed, so are our relationships and health. Let's say *yes* to rest.

1 Samuel 16:1–13
Psalm 89:20,21–22,27–28
Mark 2:23–28

Wednesday

JANUARY 21

• ST. AGNES, VIRGIN AND MARTYR •

O God, I will sing a new song to you;
a ten-stringed lyre I will chant your praise.
—PSALM 144:9

Each day there is an opportunity to sing to God in new and loving ways. In our words, actions, and attitudes we sing. In how we harmonize with one another and unite in service and solidarity, in how we build community and bless and encourage others; each action can be a type of song. And each song we sing is new because we are new people, made fresh by God's mercy and grace. Each act of love we offer can become like a symphony that proclaims the beauty of God's goodness. May it be!

1 Samuel 17:32–33,37,40–51
Psalm 144:1b,2,9–10
Mark 3:1–6

Thursday

JANUARY 22

• DAY OF PRAYER FOR THE LEGAL PROTECTION OF UNBORN CHILDREN •

Have mercy on me, O God, for men trample upon me;
all the day they press their attack against me.
— PSALM 56:2

Unfortunately, we don't have to strain to find people who are treated harshly: the vulnerable, neglected, dismissed, ignored, and attacked. Not every life is honored and protected as God intended. What if each person who is crying out to God for mercy is also crying out to us? We are part of the body of Christ and are commissioned for God's service. *God, help me to respond to the cries of the poor today with mercy, courage, and compassion. Amen.*

1 Samuel 18:6–9; 19:1–7
Psalm 56:2–3,9–10a,10b–11,12–13
Mark 3:7–12

Friday

JANUARY 23

• ST. VINCENT, DEACON AND MARTYR * ST. MARIANNE COPE, VIRGIN •

May the LORD reward you generously for what you have done this day.
—1 SAMUEL 24:19

A man sat on the sidewalk next to a fancy office building in a giant city. I watched most people rush by, ignoring his tired face and sign asking for help. Some put a coin into his cup without a word. I decided to sit next to him, ask his name, and give him attention. "Could you get me a cup of coffee?" I heard. When I came back with the steaming drink, I heard, "May God reward you for your kindness." When I went on my way, I felt certain that God already rewarded me, because I felt I had encountered God.

1 Samuel 24:3–21
Psalm 57:2,3–4,6 and 11
Mark 3:13–19

Saturday

JANUARY 24

• ST. FRANCIS DE SALES, BISHOP AND DOCTOR OF THE CHURCH •

Jesus came with his disciples into the house.
Again the crowd gathered,
making it impossible for them even to eat.
When his relatives heard of this they set out
to seize him,
for they said, "He is out of his mind."
—MARK 3:20–21

Enter into a conversation with Christ:
Jesus, it offers me comfort to know that you know what it's like to be smothered. I sometimes feel so needed by others that it's tough to take care of myself; to eat well and rest. You knew this too. Jesus, I see how you are pulled at, misunderstood, and accused. Did you feel trapped and out of control, like I sometimes do? Teach me how to handle each pressure with grace, Jesus. Help me to be like you. Amen.

2 Samuel 1:1–4,11–12,19,23–27
Psalm 80: 2–3,5–7
Mark 3:20–21

Sunday

JANUARY 25

• THIRD SUNDAY IN ORDINARY TIME •

I urge you, brothers and sisters, in the name of our Lord Jesus Christ,
that all of you agree in what you say,
and that there be no divisions among you,
but that you be united in the same mind
and in the same purpose.
—1 CORINTHIANS 1:10

St. Paul challenged the first Christians to let go of division and seek unity. God designed humankind to be rich in diversity. Differences can divide us, though, when we're judgmental and afraid of what's unfamiliar. A mature religious identity embraces differences as chances to learn, grow, and relate. As disciples of Jesus, let's say *yes* to unity. Let's be a mature community of faith.

Isaiah 8:23—9:3
Psalm 27:1,4,13–14 (1a)
1 Corinthians 1:10–13,17
Matthew 4:12–23

Monday

JANUARY 26

• ST. TIMOTHY AND ST. TITUS, BISHOPS •

Into whatever house you enter, first say,
"Peace to this household."
If a peaceful person lives there,
your peace will rest on him;
but if not, it will return to you.
—LUKE 10:5–6

Jesus calls us to oneness in our households, our parishes, and our nation. Jesus also calls us to unity within ourselves. If we say one thing but do another, then our words are not united with our actions. Our external life ought to mirror our internal life. To become a grateful person, foster a grateful heart. If you want to be patient with others, be patient with yourself. The challenge is to live with integrity.

2 Timothy 1:1–8 or Titus 1:1–5
Psalm 96:1–2a,2b–3,7–8a,10
Luke 10:1–9

Tuesday

JANUARY 27

• ST. ANGELA MERICI, VIRGIN •

When [David] finished making these offerings,
he blessed the people in the name
of the LORD of hosts.
He then distributed among all the people,
to each man and each woman in the entire
multitude of Israel,
a loaf of bread, a cut of roast meat, and a raisin cake.
—2 SAMUEL 6:18–19

Look at David's leadership. He joyfully worships God and *then* figures out a way to share the celebration with each person. His sacrifice and offering to God expand from the Ark of the Covenant out to the people of God. This is servant leadership: generous, nourishing, and focused on the other. We can be servant leaders too.

2 Samuel 6:12b–15,17–19
Psalm 24:7,8,9,10
Mark 3:31–35

Wednesday

JANUARY 28

• ST. THOMAS AQUINAS, PRIEST AND DOCTOR OF THE CHURCH •

[Jesus said,] "Those sown on rich soil are the ones who hear the word and accept it and bear fruit thirty and sixty and a hundredfold."
—MARK 4:20

When I was a young adult serving in ministry, I remember bemoaning to a mentor that I didn't know if any of my efforts were going to make a difference. Did children understand when I told Bible stories? I was uncertain if all I did to share God's love and goodness really mattered. "You are planting seeds," I was told. "You'll need to trust God that what's meant to bloom will grow." *God, deepen my trust, that efforts I exert for your glory will bear great fruit. Amen.*

2 Samuel 7:4–17
Psalm 89:4–5,27–28,29–30
Mark 4:1–20

Thursday

JANUARY 29

[David said,] "It is you, LORD of hosts, God of Israel,
who said in a revelation to your servant,
"I will build a house for you.'
Therefore your servant now finds the courage
to make this prayer to you.
And now, Lord GOD, you are God
and your words are truth;
you have made this generous promise to your servant.
Do, then, bless the house of your servant
that it may be before you forever;
for you, Lord GOD, have promised,
and by your blessing the house of your servant
shall be blessed forever."

—2 SAMUEL 7:27–29

This prayer that King David prayed to God can also be our prayer. Your prayer. My prayer. Reread these ancient words. Each of us can offer a house to God, a sacred space that honors God's promises and truth. We can give a home to God in our heart.

2 Samuel 7:18–19,24–29
Psalm 132:1–2,3–5,11,12,13–14
Mark 4:21–25

Friday

JANUARY 30

[Jesus] said,
"To what shall we compare the kingdom of God,
or what parable can we use for it?
It is like a mustard seed that, when it is sown
in the ground,
is the smallest of all the seeds on the earth.
But once it is sown, it springs up and becomes
the largest of plants
and puts forth large branches,
so that the birds of the sky can dwell in its shade."
—MARK 4:30–32

God's reign is like a tiny mustard seed that grows into a giant twelve-foot bush offering shelter and refuge. If the peace and justice of God's reign are like this, then let's contribute to its expansion. May the mustard seed grow and bring new life and hope to desolate places, including where it's least expected.

2 Samuel 11:1–4a,5–10a,13–17
Psalm 51:3–4,5–6a,6bcd–7,10–11
Mark 4:26–34

Saturday
JANUARY 31

• ST. JOHN BOSCO, PRIEST •

[Jesus] woke up,
rebuked the wind,
and said to the sea, "Quiet! Be still!"
The wind ceased and there was great calm.
—MARK 4:39

By his words and will, Jesus can control the wind and the sea. But what about each of us? When we feel anxious and stormy, Christ offers calm. To know calm may take intention, focus, or discipline. We may be required to go away to a quiet place, such as an adoration chapel. Or we can pause and breathe deeply wherever we are. Today, let's center our gaze on Christ and respond to Jesus's words: "Quiet! Be still!"

2 Samuel 12:1–7a,10–17
Psalm 51:12–13,14–15,16–17
Mark 4:35–41

Sunday

FEBRUARY 1

• FOURTH SUNDAY IN ORDINARY TIME •

God chose the foolish of the world
to shame the wise,
and God chose the weak of the world
to shame the strong,
and God chose the lowly and despised of the world,
those who count for nothing,
to reduce to nothing those who are something,
so that no human being might boast before God.
—1 CORINTHIANS 1:27–29

Since God chose the despised to shame the strong, we may want to consider with whom we tend to associate, and whom we prefer. Do we listen to the weak, broken, downtrodden, and marginalized? If we devote our time and energy to accompanying the poor, then perhaps we'll become fools for Christ.

Zephaniah 2:3; 3:12–13
Psalm 146:6–7,8–9,9–10
1 Corinthians 1:26–31
Matthew 5:1–12a

Monday

FEBRUARY 2

• THE PRESENTATION OF THE LORD •

[Simeon prayed,] "Now, Master, you may let your servant go
in peace, according to your word,
for my eyes have seen your salvation,
which you prepared in sight
of all the peoples:
a light for revelation to the Gentiles,
and glory for your people Israel."
—LUKE 2:29–32

Simeon and Anna remained faithful to their hope and trust in God's promises. They knew what they were expecting, and it was obvious to both of them when the time of fulfillment arrived. May we learn from their faith and imitate it today by leaning into hope and trust. Let's be open to seeing God's wonders, no matter how long we must wait.

Malachi 3:1–4
Psalm 24:7,8,9,10
Hebrews 2:14–18
Luke 2:22–40

Tuesday

FEBRUARY 3

• ST. BLAISE, BISHOP AND MARTYR • ST. ANSGAR, BISHOP •

She had suffered greatly at the hands of many doctors
and had spent all that she had.
Yet she was not helped but only grew worse.
She had heard about Jesus and came up
behind him in the crowd
and touched his cloak.
She said, "If I but touch his clothes, I shall be cured."
—MARK 5:26–28

At different times in our lives, each of us needs healing. We may long for cures and hope for miracles, yet healing is the real need. When Jesus healed others, he offered them restoration that brought them back into the community, from isolation to union. Some scholars say this is what salvation means: we are liberated from that which causes us to be separated from others. We are changed and connected, able to act as instruments of Christ's healing for others.

2 Samuel 18:9–10,14b,24–25a,30—19:3
Psalm 86:1–2,3–4,5–6
Mark 5:21–43

Wednesday

FEBRUARY 4

Then I acknowledged my sin to you;
my guilt I covered not.
I said, "I confess my faults to the LORD,"
and you took away the guilt of my sin.
—PSALM 32:5

We don't have to hold the ache of sorrow and sin alone. It is a grace to be part of a church that offers the Sacrament of Reconciliation, a rite wherein we admit the truth of the harm we've caused, and are heard, held, and set free. And even when we can't make it to confession, we can tell the truth to someone safe: a spiritual director, therapist, friend, doctor, minister, or loved one. God provides ways for our guilt to go away. By God's designs, we are made whole in truth telling.

2 Samuel 24:2,9–17
Psalm 32:1–2,5,6,7
Mark 6:1–6

Thursday

FEBRUARY 5

• ST. AGATHA, VIRGIN AND MARTYR •

[David said,] "Riches and honor are from you,
In your hand are power and might;
it is yours to give grandeur and strength to all."
—1 CHRONICLES 29:12

David's prayer can be our prayer too. We can acknowledge that all wealth is a gift from God—a gift to be shared. *God, help me to surrender to your power today. Whether it's the richness of relationships or material goods, help me to share the gifts you've blessed me with. Amen.*

1 Kings 2:1–4,10–12
1 Chronicles 29:10,11ab,11d–12a,12bcd
Mark 6:7–13

Friday FEBRUARY 6

• ST. PAUL MIKI AND COMPANIONS, MARTYRS •

With his whole being he loved his Maker
and daily had his praises sung;
He set singers before the altar and by their voices
he made sweet melodies.
—SIRACH 47:8–9B

Here we have a foreshadow of the great commandment: love the Lord your God with all your heart and soul, and love your neighbor as yourself (see Mark 12:30–31). This path of love is a song that we can sing wholeheartedly. Let's offer love to God and others as we sing praise.

Sirach 47:2–11
Psalm 18:31,47 and 50,51
Mark 6:14–29

Saturday

FEBRUARY 7

Give your servant, therefore, an understanding heart to judge your people and to distinguish right from wrong.

—1 KINGS 3:9

Praying for an understanding heart means staying open to a shift in perspective. To see reality the way God sees it, we may approach a challenge from a different vantage point, like an eagle that flies overhead. We may need to come close with a magnifier and study the details. We may need to close our mouths and listen to what others are saying about what's happening. With God's grace and help, we may see with clarity to distinguish what's right.

1 Kings 3:4–13
Psalm 119:9,10,11,12,13,14
Mark 6:30–34

Sunday

FEBRUARY 8

• FIFTH SUNDAY IN ORDINARY TIME •

Thus says the LORD:
Share your bread with the hungry,
shelter the oppressed and the homeless;
clothe the naked when you see them,
and do not turn your back on your own.
Then your light shall break forth like the dawn.
—ISAIAH 58:7–8

Love speaks to you:
I am light and you are mine.
I designed you to glow.
Each time you welcome a stranger, share food,
or give someone shelter,
you help others see my light.
Each act of mercy brightens the world.
Beam brightly, dear one,
and show others my love.
Thank you.

Isaiah 58:7–10
Psalm 112:4–5,6–7,8–9 (4a)
1 Corinthians 2:1–5
Matthew 5:13–16

Monday

FEBRUARY 9

May your priests be clothed with justice;
let your faithful ones shout merrily for joy.
—PSALM 132:9

When we're baptized, we become "priests, prophets, and kings," so this message is for us: we can be clothed with justice. Yet the justice of God is not what the world expects. The justice that we wear on our sleeves is concern for the little ones, the unprotected, and the suffering. As we help those who are struggling to gain a lighter load, we are filled with the joy of communal liberation.

1 Kings 8:1–7,9–13
Psalm 132:6–7,8–10
Mark 6:53–56

Tuesday

FEBRUARY 10

• ST. SCHOLASTICA, VIRGIN •

[Jesus responded,] "Well did Isaiah prophesy about you hypocrites,
as it is written:
'This people honors me with their lips,
but their hearts are far from me;
in vain do they worship me,
teaching as doctrines human precepts.'
You disregard God's commandments but cling to
human tradition."

—MARK 7:10

Speak to Jesus in prayer:

God, may I give you more than just lip service today. May I give you my heart. Through my actions, may I show you my sincere devotion and love. Please provide the graces I need to know and accept your will; may I focus on what is right and true. Amen.

1 Kings 8:22–23,27–30
Psalm 84:3,4,5 and 10,11
Mark 7:1–13

Wednesday

FEBRUARY 11

• OUR LADY OF LOURDES •

Commit to the LORD your way;
trust in him, and he will act.
He will make justice dawn for you like the light;
bright as the noonday shall be your vindication.
—PSALM 37:5–6

A packed schedule, a to-do list, a plan: we each have our own way before us. Alone with our ambitions, we can become overwhelmed. The God of all time is the Way who is available and ready to act, to accompany us and guide us along. May our hopes for the day be committed to God's way, the way of light and life.

1 Kings 10:1–10
Psalm 37:5–6,30–31,39–40
Mark 7:14–23

Thursday

FEBRUARY 12

[The woman replied,] "Lord, even the dogs under the table eat the children's scraps."
—MARK 7:28

The Syrophoenician woman in this Gospel is a mighty advocate for those who are unseen: those under tables eating scraps, invisible and neglected. Because of her voice, Jesus widens his view. This scene shows us that the impact of words can expand beyond the traps of time. We can follow her example and boldly speak up.

1 Kings 11:4–13
Psalm 106:3–4,35–36,37 and 40
Mark 7:24–30

Friday

FEBRUARY 13

They were exceedingly astonished and they said,
"He has done all things well.
He makes the deaf hear and the mute speak."
—MARK 7:37

There are times when we choose not to listen and times when we tune out. There are times when we could speak up but decide to keep our mouths closed, our voices silent. By God's grace, may we discern when to listen and when to speak well during each encounter we have.

1 Kings 11:29–32; 12:19
Psalm 81:10–11ab,12–13,14–15
Mark 7:31–37

Saturday

FEBRUARY 14

• ST. CYRIL, MONK * ST. METHODIUS, BISHOP •

Then, taking the seven loaves he gave thanks,
broke them,
and gave them to his disciples to distribute,
and they distributed them to the crowd.
—MARK 8:6

In this one verse we are offered an outline of every eucharistic act. Bread and wine are blessed and transformed in the spirit of thanksgiving. This is what we remember at each liturgy, and this is our story: We are taken, blessed, broken, and shared. In service to one another in community, through acts of compassion and kindness, we feed and are fed. By bread broken, we become one.

1 Kings 12:26–32; 13:33–34
Psalm 106:6–7ab,19–20,21–22
Mark 8:1–10

Sunday

FEBRUARY 15

• SIXTH SUNDAY IN ORDINARY TIME •

But as it is written:
"What eye has not seen, and ear has not heard,
and what has not entered the human heart,
what God has prepared for those who love him,"
this God has revealed to us through the Spirit.
For the Spirit scrutinizes everything,
even the depths of God.
—1 CORINTHIANS 2:9–10

Like the ocean, God's love is expansive and deep—blue waves extending all the way to the horizon. God is mysterious, holding currents, storms, waves, and diverse creatures. In God, there is wonder, beauty, and possibility. Bioluminescent sea creatures come to mind: little ones that glow in the dark, deep waters. Let's enter the depths of God's goodness today. Let's be ready to glow.

Sirach 15:15–20
Psalm 119:1–2,4–5,17–18,33–34 (1b)
1 Corinthians 2:6–10
Matthew 5:17–37

Monday

FEBRUARY 16

Consider it all joy, my brothers and sisters,
when you encounter various trials,
for you know that the testing of your faith
produces perseverance.
—JAMES 1:2–3

Joy in the midst of hardship: Is this a contradiction? No, turns out, it's human. We can suffer, deal with accusations and downright cruelty, yet still find joy. Joy, after all, isn't bliss or denial, it's more than being happy. Joy is spiritual contentment. No matter how tough the trials, we are strengthened by grace and continue to serve, show up, and share God's love.

James 1:1–11
Psalm 119:67,68,71,72,75,76
Mark 8:11–13

Tuesday

FEBRUARY 17

• THE SEVEN HOLY FOUNDERS OF THE SERVITE ORDER •

"Do you not yet understand or comprehend?
Are your hearts hardened?
Do you have eyes and not see, ears and not hear?"
—MARK 8:17–18

If we're honest, most of us can admit that at times we are dense: truth, wonders, and miracles are right in front of our faces, but we don't catch the clues. Our agendas and ideas easily get in the way of our being open to understanding what God reveals. Although our hearts might be hardened, we have a chance to change. *Jesus, change my heart. Amen.*

James 1:12–18
Psalm 94:12–13a,14–15,18–19
Mark 8:14–21

Wednesday

FEBRUARY 18

• ASH WEDNESDAY •

Even now, says the LORD,
return to me with your whole heart,
with fasting, and weeping, and mourning;
Rend your hearts, not your garments.
—JOEL 2:12–13

It's Ash Wednesday, the start of Lent. We will wear dirt on our faces to remember that we are needy children of God: needy for grace, mercy, and guidance. Dependent on God, we are entering a season centered on prayer, almsgiving, and fasting. These acts rearrange our lives—and help us more wholeheartedly say *yes* to loving God and neighbor with all we are. We can't do this without God's help. Amen to being needy for God's grace.

Joel 2:12–18
Psalm 51:3–4,5–6ab,12–13,14 and 17
2 Corinthians 5:20—6:2
Matthew 6:1–6,16–18

Thursday

FEBRUARY 19

• THURSDAY AFTER ASH WEDNESDAY •

[Jesus said,] "If anyone wishes to come after me,
he must deny himself
and take up his cross daily and follow me.
For whoever wishes to save his life will lose it,
but whoever loses his life for my sake will save it."
—LUKE 9:23–24

Pretty crosses decorate walls and are worn as jewelry. When Jesus tells us to take up our daily crosses and follow him, he is asking us to do something tougher than uplift religious decor. Christ calls us to consider what sort of suffering we must bear for the sake of the greater good. Could we sacrifice our ego and pride? Lent is a good time to consider how comfort zones complicate caring for others. We must let go of comfort, even if it costs us something, even if it hurts.

Deuteronomy 30:15–20
Psalm 1:1–2,3,4 and 6
Luke 9:22–25

Friday

FEBRUARY 20

• FRIDAY AFTER ASH WEDNESDAY •

[Jesus said,] "The days will come when the bridegroom
is taken away from them,
and then they will fast."
—MATTHEW 9:15

Today is the first Friday of Lent: a day for fasting. Why do we fast? We fast to remember our dependence on God. We fast because we believe that we are more than physical bodies: We believe in eternal life and that our spiritual lives are valuable. We fast so we can grow in discipline, keep our priorities in order, and make room for the graces needed to love God and neighbor. *Each time I feel hungry today, may I turn to you O God. Amen.*

Isaiah 58:1–9a
Psalm 51:3–4,5–6ab,18–19
Matthew 9:14–15

Saturday

FEBRUARY 21

• SATURDAY AFTER ASH WEDNESDAY • ST. PETER DAMIAN, BISHOP AND DOCTOR OF THE CHURCH •

[The Lord says,] "If you remove from your midst oppression,
false accusation and malicious speech;
If you bestow your bread on the hungry
and satisfy the afflicted;
Then light shall rise for you in the darkness,
and the gloom shall become for you like midday."

—ISAIAH 58:9–10

The prophet Isaiah gets it: oppression, lies, and persecution make us gloomy. As a flawed human family, we create trouble for one another. But this is only part of the story. We are gospel people, ready to proclaim the Good News—there's a way for every mouth to be fed, every human to feel dignified, and the gloom to lift. This work is our work; we are called to end oppression.

Isaiah 58:9b–14
Psalm 86:1–2,3–4,5–6
Luke 5:27–32

Sunday

FEBRUARY 22

• FIRST SUNDAY OF LENT •

The woman saw that the tree was good for food,
pleasing to the eyes, and desirable for gaining wisdom.
So she took some of its fruit and ate it;
and she also gave some to her husband,
who was with her,
and he ate it.
—GENESIS 3:6

Lent is a good time to consider the stories we tell ourselves. What is our "tree of knowledge?" We can behave like Eve and justify our disobedience to God's plan. We can easily believe that our pursuit of pleasure, possessions, or power is acceptable, even good. We can bring others into the narratives we tell so as to feel better about our choices. Yet the path toward holiness is paved with humility, sacrifice, and powerlessness. We see this on the Cross and in the holy ones we know. We have a chance to reorient ourselves in the story of our lives.

Genesis 2:7–9; 3:1–7
Psalm 51:3–4,5–6,12–13,17
Romans 5:12–19 or 5:12,17–19
Matthew 4:1–11

Monday

FEBRUARY 23

• ST. POLYCARP, BISHOP AND MARTYR •

[Jesus said,] "For I was hungry and you gave me food,
I was thirsty and you gave me drink,
a stranger and you welcomed me,
naked and you clothed me,
ill and you cared for me,
in prison and you visited me."
—MATTHEW 25:35–36

Many of us are concerned about how to get to heaven. A Scripture teacher helped me understand that this is the only passage that provides a list of needed actions. The list is not long: when we love God, we love our neighbors, and we act with mercy. Holiness and devotion are shown through outward expressions of service and kindness. Each gesture of care offers a little glimpse of heaven. Today we have an opportunity to reveal heaven to another person.

Leviticus 19:1–2,11–18
Psalm 19:8,9,10,15
Matthew 25:31–46

Tuesday

FEBRUARY 24

So shall my word be
that goes forth from my mouth;
It shall not return to me void,
but shall do my will,
achieving the end for which I sent it.
—ISAIAH 55:11

Let's converse with Christ:

Lord, I believe you are the Word: you speak forth your truth and love into the profound and the ordinary. Help me be open to the messages you are sending through every human encounter and in the busy and mundane moments. God, I invite you to always be the first message and the final word. Amen.

Isaiah 55:10–11
Psalm 34:4–5,6–7,16–17,18–19
Matthew 6:7–15

Wednesday

FEBRUARY 25

A clean heart create for me, O God,
and a steadfast spirit renew within me.
—PSALM 51:12

Today is a good day to do a little decluttering of our hearts. We have a chance to sweep out the cobwebs of selfishness. We can scrub away the grime of greed and pride. God is eager to help us become renewed and refreshed this Lent. *Come, Holy Housekeeper, clean out my heart. Amen.*

Jonah 3:1–10
Psalm 51:3–4,12–13,18–19
Luke 11:29–32

Thursday

FEBRUARY 26

Jesus said to his disciples:
"Ask and it will be given to you;
seek and you will find;
knock and the door will be opened to you."
—MATTHEW 7:7

I grew up in a family of storytellers, and this built an expectation that my friends will tell me what's happening in their lives without my prodding. This, of course, is not how everyone operates. In one of my deepest friendships, I continue to learn things that surprise me. My friend shrugs and says, "Well, you never asked." Could it be like that with Jesus? Could Jesus simply be waiting for us to ask?

Esther C:12,14–16,23–25
Psalm 138:1–2ab,2cde–3,7c–8
Matthew 7:7–12

Friday

FEBRUARY 27

• ST. GREGORY OF NAREK, ABBOT AND DOCTOR OF THE CHURCH •

[Jesus said,] "Settle with your opponent quickly while on the way to court."

—MATTHEW 5:25

When we deal with personal or legal squabbles in our lives, we may think that Jesus's instruction doesn't apply to us, that his words relate only within his historical context. Yet Jesus's words are universal: his message is relevant to every age, every people. Christ informs us that it is always better to try to settle conflict ourselves: to forgive and offer mercy. As Pope Francis has said, "A little bit of mercy makes the world less cold and more just." We are called to be like Christ; we must offer mercy.

Ezekiel 18:21–28
Psalm 130:1–2,3–4,5–7a,7bc–8
Matthew 5:20–26

Saturday

FEBRUARY 28

Moses spoke to the people, saying:
"This day the LORD, your God,
commands you to observe these statutes and decrees.
Be careful, then,
to observe them with all your heart
and with all your soul."
—DEUTERONOMY 26:16

Structure, order, laws, rules, routines: all of these methods serve a function. We gain security when systems operate with clarity. On the road, for example, every human is safer when drivers stay in lanes, obey speed limits, stop properly, and focus on traffic. We may not always appreciate it, but rules and systems keep us safe and protect our dignity. Let's honor the order that God established. Let's choose love.

Deuteronomy 26:16–19
Psalm 119:1–2,4–5,7–8
Matthew 5:43–48

Sunday
MARCH 1

• SECOND SUNDAY OF LENT •

Beloved:
Bear your share of hardship for the gospel
with the strength that comes from God.

He saved us and called us to a holy life,
not according to our works
but according to his own design
and the grace bestowed on us in Christ Jesus.
—2 TIMOTHY 1:8–9

Good things come at a great price. Holiness and love come with sacrifice. Being a disciple of Christ Jesus means we surrender our will. Gospel service requires us to move out of our comfort zones. Little by little, as we cooperate with God's designs and receive God's grace, we become the people God made us to be.

Genesis 12:1–4a
Psalm 33:4–5,18–19,20,22
2 Timothy 1:8b–10
Matthew 17:1–9

Monday MARCH 2

Jesus said to his disciples:
"Be merciful, just as your Father is merciful."
—LUKE 6:36

Here is a Christian pathway: showing mercy, in imitation of the one who created us. This means we offer compassion, forgiveness, help, and our hearts. The idea here isn't to neglect our needs, but to center relationships and care for the other. There's much that's great about this pathway, including the impact that it has on us. We are instruments of mercy, and the service we offer changes our hearts.

Daniel 9:4b–10
Psalm 79:8,9,11 and 13
Luke 6:36–38

Tuesday MARCH 3

• ST. KATHARINE DREXEL, VIRGIN •

[Jesus said,] "The greatest among you must be your servant.
Whoever exalts himself will be humbled;
but whoever humbles himself will be exalted."
—MATTHEW 23:12

Humility is the stuff of saints. Those who are humble are content with being simple and small, yes, but more important, they live in the truth. They are self-aware and can readily admit their strengths and weaknesses. They know who they are and feel no need to prove their worth to others. Let's look in the mirror and ask God to show us who we truly are, so we can authentically be ourselves and reveal to the world that we are children of God, full of great dignity and light.

Isaiah 1:10,16–20
Psalm 50:8–9,16bc–17,21 and 23
Matthew 23:1–12

But my trust is in you, O LORD;
I say, "You are my God."
In your hands is my destiny; rescue me
from the clutches of my enemies and my persecutors.
—PSALM 31:14–15

Today is a good day to show others that we trust in God. May our behavior speak a message that says we know we have a higher power, that we are dependent on God's might. May our attitudes, words, and interactions say something about our belief that God's got us. God's handling the tough stuff.

Jeremiah 18:18–20
Psalm 31:5–6,14,15–16
Matthew 20:17–28

Thursday

MARCH 5

More tortuous than all else is the human heart,
beyond remedy; who can understand it?
I, the LORD, alone probe the mind
and test the heart,
To reward everyone according to his ways,
according to the merits of his deeds.
—JEREMIAH 17:9–10

When our hearts are united with Christ, we're more likely to be united with others in their suffering. Perhaps God, who sees into our hearts, is hoping that our devotion is both internal and external: we contemplate and act. In prayer and service, we follow the God who lives deep in our hearts and knows the needs of a suffering world. Let's look for chances to unite our hearts with those who are suffering.

Jeremiah 17:5–10
Psalm 1:1–2,3,4 and 6
Luke 16:19–31

[Judah said,] "After all, he is our brother, our own flesh."
—GENESIS 37:27

Our faith tradition teaches that we are all sinners and we are all saints. Sometimes we inflict harm on others, and sometimes we are agents of healing. Much of our life is lived in the tension of knowing both sides of who we are. The challenge, though, is to not let our weaknesses define us, nor to inflate our greatness too much. To stay centered in Christ, in the right reality, try to notice what connects us to other people, to see the truth of our fraternity. Seeing all humans as siblings, we can connect with grace.

Genesis 37:3–4,12–13a,17b–28a
Psalm 105:16–17,18–19,20–21
Matthew 21:33–43,45–46

Saturday MARCH 7

• ST. PERPETUA AND ST. FELICITY, MARTYRS •

You will cast into the depths of the sea all our sins.
—MICAH 7:19

During this Lenten season of penance, it can be easy to feel awful about how we fall short. Maybe you are fasting from chocolate but forgot and ate a whole candy bar. Maybe you meant to start every day with extra prayer but slept through your alarm. Although we may be aware of how we could do better, there is no need to feel shame. God loves to forgive. God loves to help us have fresh starts. It's a grace to be dependent on God's mercy in order to grow into who we're meant to be.

Micah 7:14–15,18–20
Psalm 103:1–2,3–4,9–10,11–12
Luke 15:1–3,11–32

Sunday MARCH 8

• THIRD SUNDAY OF LENT •

In those days, in their thirst for water,
the people grumbled against Moses,
saying, "Why did you ever make us leave Egypt?"
—EXODUS 17:3

Indigenous societies declare that water is life. St. Francis of Assisi knew water as a sister: an element in the fraternal community, sacred to many species. The Israelites in the desert on their way to the Promised Land grumbled about what they lacked, perhaps forgetting that they crossed through water to freedom. And the thirst of the Samaritan woman was quenched by Christ, the Living Water. During this Lenten season, may our penance and prayers increase our gratitude for water and foster actions to protect all sacred water. And, Christ is Living Water. Give thanks for water today: vitality, sister, strength, and freedom to quench our thirst.

Exodus 17:3–7
Psalm 95:1–2,6–7,8–9 (8)
Romans 5:1–2,5–8
John 4:5–42

Monday MARCH 9

• ST. FRANCES OF ROME, RELIGIOUS •

"If the prophet had told you to do something extraordinary,
would you not have done it?"
—2 KINGS 5:13

Prophets are those who speak truths that we don't want to hear. They challenge and provoke, inviting us into collective transformation for the sake of God's will. Just as in biblical times, prophets are speaking to us now and inviting us to do extraordinary acts. We can listen and respond so as to help God's justice be known. We can do extraordinary acts of love in God's name.

2 Kings 5:1–15ab
Psalm 42:2,3; 43:3,4
Luke 4:24–30

Tuesday MARCH 10

But with contrite heart and humble spirit
let us be received.
—DANIEL 3:39

Love speaks to you:
dear one, I know.
I know the sorrow of your sin because I am with you
in the ache.
And, in your sorrow and ache, I see a beautiful longing to
change, to be better.
I welcome this.
And I welcome you into my loving arms.
Cry into my shoulder and let me hold your heartache.
I am eager to heal you and help you along.

Daniel 3:25,34–43
Psalm 25:4–5ab,6 and 7bc,8–9
Matthew 18:21–35

Wednesday

MARCH 11

[Jesus said,] "I have come not to abolish [the law] but to fulfill."
—MATTHEW 5:17

Amazingly, Jesus Christ doesn't cancel out the past; he integrates it. He takes the traditions of his ancestors and weaves them into what's emerging and fresh, creating a brand-new tapestry of loving salvation. Maybe today is a day when we'll be able to see the threads of time moving us into greater transformation and freedom. Maybe today we'll see a fulfillment of God's love.

Deuteronomy 4:1,5–9
Psalm 147:12–13,15–16,19–20
Matthew 5:17–19

Thursday
MARCH 12

Come, let us bow down in worship;
let us kneel before the LORD who made us.
—PSALM 95:6

Prayer is much more than a mental act. In our postures and gestures we give God our attention and respect. We kneel, bow, genuflect, and stand to show God honor. We fold our hands in prayer and sing out praise. With our bodies, we reverence our awesome God who made us and loves us without condition.

Jeremiah 7:23–28
Psalm 95:1–2,6–7,8–9
Luke 11:14–23

Friday

MARCH 13

I will heal their defection, says the LORD,
I will love them freely;
for my wrath is turned away from them.
—HOSEA 14:5

It's another Lenten Friday, a day to remember to love God and neighbor through acts of almsgiving, prayer, and fasting. We don't do these actions to earn God's love, for God's love is already freely given. We do acts of penance because God's love is overflowing and we are God's body. With our help, others can have food, resources, and care.

Hosea 14:2–10
Psalm 81:6c–8a,8bc–9,10–11ab,14 and 17
Mark 12:28–34

Saturday

MARCH 14

[The tax collector prayed,] "O God, be merciful to me a sinner."
—LUKE 18:13

In this parable of the Pharisee and the tax collector, we encounter a tax collector who teaches us how to pray and how to be honest about who we are. It is Jesus who frees us from what could burden us. We can ponder Christ's mercy as we meditate on the meaning of the Jesus Prayer: *Lord Jesus Christ, Son of God, have mercy on me, a sinner*. This simple prayer can become a mantra for us, a statement we repeat to stay humble as we move through our day.

Hosea 6:1–6
Psalm 51:3–4,18–19,20–21ab
Luke 18:9–14

Live as children of light,
for light produces every kind of goodness
and righteousness and truth.
—EPHESIANS 5:8–9

It's the fourth Sunday in Lent, the halfway mark through the Lenten season and a day of Sabbath. As you rest today, take some time to check in. Consider your Lenten intentions, hopes, and prayers, and observe how Christ is bringing goodness to light. Perhaps you're gaining insight into how dependent you are on God, how much you need God's grace. Pause and notice what God is doing in your life this Lent.

1 Samuel 16:1b,6–7,10–13a
Psalm 23:1–3a,3b–4,5,6 (1)
Ephesians 5:8–14
John 9:1–41

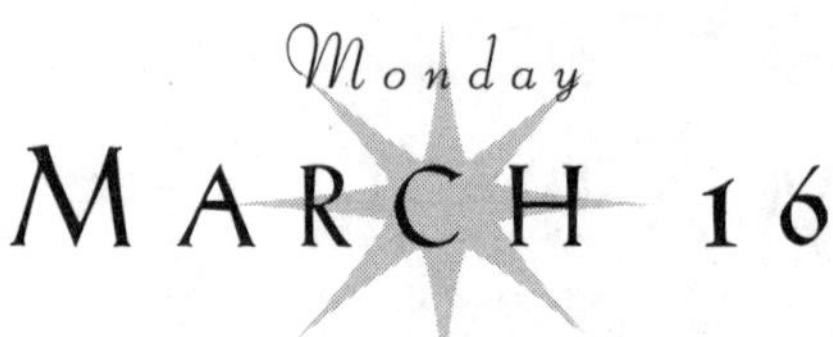

Monday
MARCH 16

Lo, I am about to create a new heavens and a new earth.
—ISAIAH 65:17

Lent is a word that comes from an Old English word for "spring season," and for those of us in the northern hemisphere, we celebrate the season of Lent while springtime surrounds. New life is sprouting forth through the thawing earth, new buds are forming, and migrating birds have returned from their visits to warmer climates. Likewise, our Lenten practices open new space for God to reach into our hearts and create us anew. Give thanks to God who makes all things new.

Isaiah 65:17–21
Psalm 30:2 and 4,5–6,11–12a and 13b
John 4:43–54

Tuesday MARCH 17

• ST. PATRICK, BISHOP •

[Jesus asked,] "Do you want to be well?"
—JOHN 5:6

Jesus's question to the disabled man in the pool near the Jerusalem Sheep Gate is also a question for each of us. Jesus's voice is gentle. His curiosity is sincere. If we are ready to be well, we may need to say *yes* to being made well. We may need to get ready to pick up our mats and walk.

Ezekiel 47:1–9,12
Psalm 46:2–3,5–6,8–9
John 5:1–16

Wednesday

MARCH 18

• ST. CYRIL OF JERUSALEM, BISHOP AND DOCTOR OF THE CHURCH •

The LORD lifts up all who are falling
and raises up all who are bowed down.
—PSALM 145:14

We are called to act. Let's begin with prayer:
God, help me to reach out and offer comfort to others today. Provide for me the graces and strength I need to serve and tend to your people. I'm willing to be your hands and feet, Good God. May my hands and heart be open and ready to give and receive. Make me totally yours. Amen.

Isaiah 49:8–15
Psalm 145:8–9,13cd–14,17–18
John 5:17–30

Thursday

MARCH 19

• ST. JOSEPH, SPOUSE OF THE BLESSED VIRGIN MARY •

"It is he who shall build a house for my name.
And I will make his royal throne firm forever.
I will be a father to him,
and he shall be a son to me.
Your house and your kingdom shall endure forever
before me;
your throne shall stand firm forever."
—2 SAMUEL 7:13–14,16

It's the Feast of St. Joseph, a joyous day for us to contemplate the mysteries of God's plan. As brothers and sisters in Christ, we are part of the Holy Family, members of a spiritual lineage of grace. Like St. Joseph, we can say *yes* to humbly loving those whom God puts in our lives. Like St. Joseph, we can help more people to know the safety of belonging, of being at home.

2 Samuel 7:4–5a,12–14a,16
Psalm 89:2–3,4–5,27 and 29
Romans 4:13,16–18,22
Matthew 1:16,18–21,24a or Luke 2:41–51a

Friday MARCH 20

The LORD is close to the brokenhearted;
and those who are crushed in spirit he saves.
—PSALM 34:19

Each of us knows the anguish of disappointment, rejection, and grief. At one time or another, we feel how much it costs to really care. Heartbreak is human, and God knows it too. Consider the Cross, and how heartbroken Christ must have felt. And yet, we know that the Cross isn't the end of the story. With God, there's a way through the pain that leads to great freedom.

Wisdom 2:1a,12–22
Psalm 34:17–18,19–20,21 and 23
John 7:1–2,10,25–30

Saturday

MARCH 21

"Does our law condemn a man before it first hears him and finds out what he is doing?"
—JOHN 7:51

The Pharisee Nicodemus referred to his faith tradition to challenge others to be more compassionate and open-minded, advocating for Jesus. Our faith tradition can inform us about how to advocate for the persecuted too. Let's look around our faith communities and notice how our faith tradition can offer strength to all.

Jeremiah 11:18–20
Psalm 7:2–3,9bc–10,11–12
John 7:40–53

Sunday
MARCH 22

• FIFTH SUNDAY OF LENT •

Jesus told her,
"I am the resurrection and the life;
whoever believes in me, even if he dies, will live,
and everyone who lives and believes in me
will never die."
—JOHN 11:25–26

During Lent, we remember who we are: people of life who are called to say *yes* to all that gives life and shares life. Jesus tells us that if we believe in him, we will be freed from death. This is a mystery, and it is true. We choose life again and again each time we choose to be centered in loving God and neighbor. By each act of care and kindness, we say *yes* to life, to becoming who God made us to be. We show that we believe.

Ezekiel 37:12–14
Psalm 130:1–2,3–4,5–6,7–8
Romans 8:8–11
John 11:1–45

• ST. TURIBIUS OF MOGROVEJO, BISHOP •

"Go, and from now on do not sin any more."
—JOHN 8:11

When we are forgiven, it's as if God picks us up, holds us in our sorrow, cleans us, then resituates us on the path with our feet pointing in the right direction. I can practically feel Jesus lovingly patting me on the back and offering me gentle encouragement, "Go this way now. Don't go back there." Made new by Christ's mercy, we journey onward, feeling a lightness in our step. Today, experience the joy of a restart.

Daniel 13:1–9,15–17,19–30,33–62 or 13:41c–62
Psalm 23:1–3a,3b–4,5,6
John 8:1–11

Tuesday MARCH 24

O LORD, hear my prayer,
and let my cry come to you.
Hide not your face from me
in the day of my distress.
Incline your ear to me;
in the day when I call, answer me speedily.
—PSALM 102:2–3

Lenten conversion is a time to be real about who we are, to wake up and admit how we struggle. Faces are peeled off of pillows. Masks are shed. Shields come down. We step out of hiding. We moan in discomfort and cry out to God for help. With each vulnerable gesture, we are accepting reality. We are opening our hearts wider to God's love.

Numbers 21:4–9
Psalm 102:2–3,16–18,19–21
John 8:21–30

Wednesday

MARCH 25

• THE ANNUNCIATION OF THE LORD •

The angel Gabriel was sent from God
to a town of Galilee called Nazareth,
to a virgin betrothed to a man named Joseph,
of the house of David,
and the virgin's name was Mary.
And coming to her, he said,
"Hail, full of grace! The Lord is with you."
But she was greatly troubled at what was said
and pondered what sort of greeting this might be.
—LUKE 1:26–29

On this feast day, let us pray in gratitude for Mary's *yes* to God's will, for her *yes* to holiness and God's grace. We can join the angel Gabriel in his loving greeting with every Hail Mary and Rosary that helps us remember how the Blessed Virgin Mary knows what it's like to be human and what it's like to be afraid. Pray with Mary today.

Isaiah 7:10–14; 8:10
Psalm 40:7–8a,8b–9,10,11
Hebrews 10:4–10
Luke 1:26–38

Thursday
MARCH 26

Recall the wondrous deeds that he has wrought.
—PSALM 105:5

Lent can become a litany of prayerful words: recall, restore, renew, recognize, revive, reveal. Each "re" prefix offers a suggestion of where our acts of prayer, fasting, and almsgiving could bring us: back to where we started. We return to our maker, to God who made us to be loving, healthy, connected, and free. God restored our ancestors, and God is remaking us. Let us recall and rejoice.

Genesis 17:3–9
Psalm 105:4–5,6–7,8–9
John 8:51–59

Friday MARCH 27

Sing to the LORD,
praise the LORD,
For he has rescued the life of the poor
from the power of the wicked!
—JEREMIAH 20:13

A man worked in a food pantry and delighted in greeting strangers and distributing boxes and bags of groceries. When the governor came to visit, the man thanked her for the support and told her that he hoped the food pantry would soon be closed. The governor was confused. Why would anyone want the food pantry to close? When there's justice there will no longer be a need, the man explained. Sometimes improvements can disturb the status quo. Let's recognize the opportunity for more good.

Jeremiah 20:10–13
Psalm 18:2–3a,3bc–4,5–6,7
John 10:31–42

Saturday
MARCH 28

I will make with them a covenant of peace;
it shall be an everlasting covenant with them,
and I will multiply them, and put my sanctuary
among them forever.
—EZEKIEL 37:26

Today, look for peace. The hungry are fed, forgiveness is offered, decisions are made that put things in the right order: all of these are pathways to peace. God has promised us peace, and we may not need to search too far to notice how peace dwells with us here and now. We can notice the goodness ripple outward.

Ezekiel 37:21–28
Jeremiah 31:10,11–12abcd,13
John 11:45–56

Sunday MARCH 29

• PALM SUNDAY OF THE PASSION OF THE LORD •

The very large crowd spread their cloaks on the road,
while others cut branches from the trees
and strewed them on the road.
The crowds preceding him and those following
kept crying out and saying:
"Hosanna to the Son of David;
blessed is the he who comes in the name of the Lord;
hosanna in the highest."
—MATTHEW 21:8–9

Today, we'll gather in churches, wave our palms, and remember Jesus's grand entrance into Jerusalem. As we celebrate the joy of Palm Sunday today and the hope in Jesus Christ that this day signifies, it may be worthwhile to reflect on how we celebrate people such as athletes, artists, performers, and public servants. If Christ is our priority every day, how could we go out of our way to celebrate our hope in him?

PROCESSION:
Matthew 21:1–11

MASS:
Isaiah 50:4–7
Psalm 22:8–9,17–18,19–20,23–24 (2a)
Philippians 2:6–11
Matthew 26:14—27:66

Monday MARCH 30

• MONDAY OF HOLY WEEK •

Mary took a liter of costly perfumed oil
made from genuine aromatic nard
and anointed the feet of Jesus and dried them
with her hair.
—JOHN 12:3

It's Monday of Holy Week, a good time to become deeply immersed in the stories of Jesus's journey in Jerusalem before his Death. Notice how different characters respond to Jesus. Consider who you're relating to most right now. Perhaps Mary could be a model for you today. Maybe her generous and tender gesture of honoring Jesus has something to say about how to love, how to pray.

Isaiah 42:1–7
Psalm 27:1,2,3,13–14
John 12:1–11

I will make you a light to the nations,
that my salvation may reach to the ends of the earth.
—ISAIAH 49:6

Let's look around today and see the salvation of God illuminating the earth. Tiny fleas and herds of buffalo experience wholeness and belonging. Each time a creature thrives or a human flourishes, God is blessing a suffering planet and people with healing and grace. This is part of what salvation means. Let's help more goodness come to light. When we do, we'll make God's salvation known.

Isaiah 49:1–6
Psalm 71:1–2,3–4a,5ab–6ab,15 and 17
John 13:21–33,36–38

Wednesday APRIL 1

• WEDNESDAY OF HOLY WEEK •

One of the Twelve, who was called Judas Iscariot,
went to the chief priests and said,
"What are you willing to give me
if I hand him over to you?"
—MATTHEW 26:14–15

Greed complicates our lives and burdens our common home, Earth. We may never know for sure, but it seems likely that greed was a motive for Judas when he chose to turn Jesus over to the authorities. Yet greed need not trap us. We have an antidote to negativity and sin: compassionate generosity. As we prepare to approach the Triduum, we can choose to respond to hardship with hope, and to manipulation with truth.

Isaiah 50:4–9a
Psalm 69:8–10,21–22,31 and 33–34
Matthew 26:14–25

Thursday
APRIL 2

• THURSDAY OF HOLY WEEK (HOLY THURSDAY) •

[Jesus said,] "Do this, as often as you drink it, in remembrance of me." For as often as you eat this bread and drink the cup, you proclaim the death of the Lord until he comes.
—1 CORINTHIANS 11:25–26

Have you ever been with someone approaching the end of their life? Did you listen more closely to every word they uttered? Did everything they say seem to matter more? It must have been like this for Jesus's disciples at the Last Supper. They didn't know what was ahead, but they could feel that things were shifting. What a grace that he taught them to break bread and drink wine in remembrance of him. Even for us, it is simple, sacred, and holy to share meals and remember our friend Jesus.

CHRISM MASS:
Isaiah 61:1–3a,6a,8b–9
Psalm 89:21–22,25,27
Revelation 1:5–8
Luke 4:16–21

EVENING MASS OF THE LORD'S SUPPER:
Exodus 12:1–8,11–14
Psalm 116:12–13,15–16bc,17–18
1 Corinthians 11:23–26
John 13:1–15

Friday APRIL 3

• FRIDAY OF THE PASSION OF THE LORD (GOOD FRIDAY) •

So they took Jesus, and, carrying the cross himself,
he went out to what is called the Place of the Skull,
in Hebrew, Golgotha.
There they crucified him, and with him two others,
one on either side, with Jesus in the middle.
—JOHN 19:16–18

Our Savior Jesus—innocent and selfless—carried the Cross, an instrument of torture, to his own execution. He modeled for us how true sacrificial love requires surrendering to suffering. He wasn't alone in his pain and horror, and his companions were common criminals. Even in his Death he remained a teacher, showing us how to allow God's graces to flow in the worst of circumstances.

Isaiah 52:13—53:12
Psalm 31:2,6,12–13,15–16,17, 25
Hebrews 4:14–16; 5:7–9
John 18:1—19:42

Saturday APRIL 4

• HOLY SATURDAY •

[The angel said,] "Do not be afraid!
I know that you are seeking Jesus the crucified.
He is not here, for he has been raised just as he said.
Come and see the place where he lay.
Then go quickly and tell his disciples."
—MATTHEW 28:5–7

Tonight, the global church will remember all of salvation history: how God created the mysteries of the universe and made a covenant with humans, how we are people on a journey. And we will hear the words the angel spoke at Jesus's empty tomb. The message is: choose courage over fear, take in the truth, and share the Good News. Christ is risen! Alleluia!

VIGIL:
Genesis 1:1—2:2 or 1:1,26–31a
Psalm 104:1–2,5–6,10,12,13–14,24,35 or 33:4–5,6–7,12–13,20–22 (5b)
Genesis 22:1–18 or 22:1–2,9a,10–13,15–18
Psalm 16:5,8,9–10,11 (1)
Exodus 14:15—15:1
Exodus 15:1–2,3–4,5–6,17–18 (1b)
Isaiah 54:5–14
Psalm 30:2,4,5–6,11–12,13 (2a)
Isaiah 55:1–11
Isaiah 12:2–3,4,5–6 (3)
Baruch 3:9–15,32—4:4
Psalm 19:8,9,10,11
Ezekiel 36:16–17a,18–28
Psalm 42:3,5; 43:3,4 or Isaiah 12:2–3,4bcd,5–6 or Psalm 51:12–13,14–15,18–19
Romans 6:3–11
Psalm 118:1–2,16–17,22–23
Matthew 28:1–10

Sunday APRIL 5

• EASTER SUNDAY OF THE RESURRECTION OF THE LORD •

Brothers and sisters:
Do you not know that a little yeast leavens all the dough?
Clear out the old yeast,
so that you may become a fresh batch of dough,
inasmuch as you are unleavened.
—1 CORINTHIANS 5:6–7

Alleluia! Christ is risen! And we are risen too! The Bread of Life is our brother, and through the Resurrection, Ascension, and Holy Eucharist, we are part of his body. With this joyous Easter we are given a fresh new start to rise up and give life to others, to nourish those who are seeking belonging with hospitality and kindness, to feed those who are physically and spiritually hungry, to clear out what is old and expired, and to open our hearts wider to God's grace. Alleluia!

Acts 10:34a,37–43
Psalm 118:1–2,16–17,22–23 (24)
Colossians 3:1–4 or 1 Corinthians 5:6b–8
John 20:1–9 or Matthew 28:1–10 or, at an afternoon or evening Mass, Luke 24:13–35

Monday APRIL 6

• MONDAY WITHIN THE OCTAVE OF EASTER •

God raised this Jesus;
of this we are all witnesses.
—ACTS 2:32

It's Easter Monday: another day to dwell in the joy of the Resurrection. The apostles saw the awesomeness of the Resurrection with their own eyes; they witnessed the wonder. All these years later, giving and being a witness remains an important act for Christians. You can give witness and be a witness. Be among those who are boldly living out their faith. Be ready to witness wonder.

Acts 2:14,22–33
Psalm 16:1–2a and 5,7–8,9–10,11
Matthew 28:8–15

Tuesday APRIL 7

• TUESDAY WITHIN THE OCTAVE OF EASTER •

Mary went and announced to the disciples,
"I have seen the Lord,"
and then reported what he had told her.
—JOHN 20:18

As far as we know, Mary didn't hesitate to tell others the good news. Doubt didn't get in the way of her confidence or her message. Her voice was used for good, and a new religious movement was born: Christianity. In the spirit of Easter, we too can proclaim good news. Let's point out what's good and beautiful. Let's encourage one another and give praise, compliments, and thanks. As we do, maybe we'll help others see the Lord.

Acts 2:36–41
Psalm 33:4–5,18–19,20 and 22
John 20:11–18

Wednesday APRIL 8

• WEDNESDAY WITHIN THE OCTAVE OF EASTER •

Peter said, "I have neither silver nor gold,
but what I do have I give you:
in the name of Jesus Christ the Nazorean,
rise and walk."
—ACTS 3:6

When I taught the Acts of the Apostles to ninth graders, I gave my students an assignment to create a comic strip showing how the apostles were given the grace to do amazing things through Jesus's name. I loved grading those assignments and seeing the colorful ways students would tell the stories. If the name of Jesus was included in the storytelling, my students earned an A. Here's a possibility for everyone: by God's grace, Jesus's name is the closest thing we have to a superpower.

Acts 3:1–10
Psalm 105:1–2,3–4,6–7,8–9
Luke 24:13–35

Thursday APRIL 9

• THURSDAY WITHIN THE OCTAVE OF EASTER •

When Peter saw this, he addressed the people,
"You children of Israel, why are you amazed at this,
and why do you look so intently at us?"
—ACTS 3:12

Peter stood up and confronted the doubt around him. He understood that we may doubt the good that's hiding in plain sight. We have a holy opportunity to notice what is good—generous gestures, gentle transformations—even when doubters are loud and negative. Let's honor the good that's all around.

Acts 3:11–26
Psalm 8:2ab and 5,6–7,8–9
Luke 24:35–48

Friday
APRIL 10

• FRIDAY WITHIN THE OCTAVE OF EASTER •

Jesus came over and took the bread and gave it to them,
and in like manner the fish.
This was now the third time Jesus was revealed
to his disciples
after being raised from the dead.
—JOHN 21:13–14

It's awesome really: our God became human, died, rose, and then chose to do humble and ordinary acts, like feed people. Today, Jesus is with us in ordinary acts like eating, too. His love is felt in meals and in community. The mundane is made sacred. This awesome reality ought to define and direct us. We, too, can reveal Christ and share his love by feeding people.

Acts 4:1–12
Psalm 118:1–2 and 4,22–24,25–27a
John 21:1–14

Saturday
APRIL 11

• SATURDAY WITHIN THE OCTAVE OF EASTER •

[Peter and John said,] "It is impossible for us not to speak about what we have seen and heard."

—ACTS 4:20

I once worked with a teacher who started every class by inviting each pupil to say something good. Students were challenged to tell a story or name a miracle. This practice formed the students: They got in the habit of noticing what was good in their lives. Before long, they could notice and name how God is active in the world. Maybe the students gradually understood what was impossible: keeping quiet about what's good.

Acts 4:13–21
Psalm 118:1 and 14–15ab,16–18,19–21
Mark 16:9–15

Sunday APRIL 12

• SECOND SUNDAY OF EASTER (OR SUNDAY OF DIVINE MERCY) •

All who believed were together and had all things
in common;
they would sell their property and possessions
and divide them among all according to
each one's need.
—ACTS 2:44–45

For centuries, faithful communities have been inspired by the description of the early Christians tending to everyone's needs and sharing all things in common. Visit a monastery or ask any vowed religious: there is a freedom found in having no private possessions. No matter our vocation, every Christian is called to be communal, to share with others who believe.

Acts 2:42–47
Psalm 118:2–4,13–15,22–24 (1)
1 Peter 1:3–9
John 20:19–31

Monday

APRIL 13

• ST. MARTIN I, POPE AND MARTYR •

[Jesus said,] "The wind blows where it wills,
and you can hear the sound it makes,
but you do not know where it comes from
or where it goes;
so it is with everyone who is born of the Spirit."
—JOHN 3:8

Consider the wind: Gentle breezes refresh and foster life, while fierce winds destroy and damage. We praise God for the wonder of wind. Consider people who are full of the Spirit, their whimsy, playfulness, courage, and strength. We praise God for people filled with the Spirit, who inspire openness, freedom, and joy each time they blow through and make us new.

Acts 4:23–31
Psalm 2:1–3,4–7a,7b–9
John 3:1–8

Tuesday APRIL 14

Your decrees are worthy of trust indeed:
holiness befits your house,
O LORD, *for length of days.*
—PSALM 93:5

Imagine a world that reflected belief in God's trustworthy order. Imagine a society that cooperated with God's designs. The weak would have all they need. Jails could go out of business. Maybe every home would have a generous open-door policy. We can imagine it, but God's counting on us to animate his vision for all creation. Let's make trust in God our main business today.

Acts 4:32–37
Psalm 93:1ab,1cd–2,5
John 3:7b–15

Wednesday
APRIL 15

God so loved the world that he gave his
only-begotten Son,
so that everyone who believes in him
might not perish
but might have eternal life.
—JOHN 3:16

There's a reason why this verse is memorized by many. This one passage succinctly declares the awesome Christian message: God loves us. God became one of us. We are invited to be Christian disciples, and there are advantages to saying *yes* to God's love. We're part of this story, and we live the message each time we say *yes* to love.

Acts 5:17–26
Psalm 34:2–3,4–5,6–7,8–9
John 3:16–21

Thursday APRIL 16

But Peter and the Apostles said in reply,
"We must obey God rather than men."
—ACTS 5:29

Today could be a day for our choices to be aligned with God's will. Here's how: turn away from trends, and choose time with a loved one. Instead of seeking to please people, praise God. Forget popularity and comfort; pick justice and compassion. God's law of love is a great guide.

Acts 5:27–33
Psalm 34:2 and 9,17–18,19–20
John 3:31–36

Then Jesus took the loaves, gave thanks,
and distributed them to those who were reclining,
and also as much of the fish as they wanted.
When they had had their fill, he said to his disciples,
"Gather the fragments left over,
so that nothing will be wasted."
—JOHN 6:11–12

The God of abundance provided for the hungry who were reclining and feasting with Jesus and the disciples, just as the God of abundance provides for us now. When abundance and gratitude, rather than scarcity, guide our mindsets, motives, and actions, we can be generous instead of fearful. We know there will be plenty, and we know that there are always reasons to give thanks. By the grace of an abundant God, may we be free from wasting today.

Acts 5:34–42
Psalm 27:1,4,13–14
John 6:1–15

Saturday

APRIL 18

When they had rowed about three or four miles,
they saw Jesus walking on the sea and coming
near the boat,
and they began to be afraid.
But he said to them, "It is I. Do not be afraid."
—JOHN 6:19–20

Years ago, I slept on the couch in a Catholic Worker house on a disgustingly hot night. The workers told me to keep the front and back doors open so that a breeze could blow through the house and keep me cool, then went to their bedrooms. So when the door opened in the middle of the night, I screamed in terror, thinking an intruder had walked into the house. I couldn't see who it was without my glasses. Before I knew it, my friend's gentle voice said, "Don't be afraid; it's me. You're okay," then held me and calmed me down. Jesus did the same for his friends who were spooked. Let's imitate Christ today and help others to feel safe.

Acts 6:1–7
Psalm 33:1–2,4–5,18–19
John 6:16–21

Sunday APRIL 19

• THIRD SUNDAY OF EASTER •

Therefore my heart is glad and my soul rejoices,
my body, too, abides in confidence.

It's another Easter Sunday: the third in this joyous season! Choose joy today. Choose to feel the gladness of love deep in your bones. Allow joy to shift how you walk and how you stand strong in Christ. We are free, and we can have confidence in God's goodness. Alleluia!

Acts 2:14,22–33
Psalm 16:1–2,5,7–8,9–10,11 (11a)
1 Peter 1:17–21
Luke 24:13–35

Monday
April 20

The way of truth I have chosen;
I have set your ordinances before me.
—Psalm 119:30

In an age of misinformation and manipulation, we are offered an alternative: the way of truth. On the path of discipleship, the stepping stones are facts, honesty, and sincerity. God takes our hands and gently leads us forward as we say *yes* to what's real. When we accept what's real, we're walking toward justice and love. This is gospel living.

Acts 6:8–15
Psalm 119:23–24,26–27,29–30
John 6:22–29

Tuesday APRIL 21

• ST. ANSELM, BISHOP AND DOCTOR OF THE CHURCH •

Jesus said to them, "I am the bread of life;
whoever comes to me will never hunger,
and whoever believes in me will never thirst."
—JOHN 6:35

Physical and spiritual hungers influence how we construct our days. Desire directs the human heart and the choices we make—what we eat, how we spend our time, and how we spend our money. Jesus redirects. He says that he is ready to satisfy, feed, nourish, and strengthen. Let us believe. Let us center our choices on the Bread of Life.

Acts 7:51—8:1a
Psalm 31:3cd–4,6 and 7b and 8a,17 and 21ab
John 6:30–35

Devout men buried Stephen and made a loud lament over him.

—ACTS 8:2

When we are devoted to love—to building up a loving community and caring for one another—there are times when such devotion can lead to suffering. When this happens, it helps to know that our laments can be holy acts. It can be a form of prayer to cry and groan, to pour out our heartaches to the God of love.

Acts 8:1b–8
Psalm 66:1–3a,4–5,6–7a
John 6:35–40

Thursday

APRIL 23

• ST. GEORGE, MARTYR * ST. ADALBERT, BISHOP AND MARTYR •

Philip ran up and heard him reading Isaiah
the prophet and said,
"Do you understand what you are reading?"
He replied,
"How can I, unless someone instructs me?"
—ACTS 8:30–31

Every day we may encounter others who are curious about our faith tradition but who have never been introduced to the basics of Christianity. Let's be ready to share our faith and bear witness to how we love and share kindness. And, when needed, let's be ready to explain our beliefs and welcome those people to our faith community.

Acts 8:26–40
Psalm 66:8–9,16–17,20
John 6:44–51

Friday
APRIL 24

• ST. FIDELIS OF SIGMARINGEN, PRIEST AND MARTYR •

[Jesus said,] "For my Flesh is true food,
and my Blood is true drink.
Whoever eats my Flesh and drinks my Blood
remains in me and I in him."
—JOHN 6:55–56

Christ speaks to you:
My beloved,
I want to be close to you.
I want to nourish and strengthen you.
I want to be your food for your journey,
to enliven how you show others my love.
Receive me, love, so that I can be part of you:
so we can be one and
when others meet you, they can know my love.

Acts 9:1–20
Psalm 117:1bc,2
John 6:52–59

Saturday APRIL 25

• ST. MARK, EVANGELIST •

Be sober and vigilant.
Your opponent the Devil is prowling around
like a roaring lion
looking for someone to devour.
—1 PETER 5:8

St. Ignatius of Loyola taught the first members of the Society of Jesus to pray a daily *examen* to notice the interior patterns they felt during the day: times of consolation (experiences of grace that draw us to love, influenced by "good spirits") and times of desolation (times of spiritual confusion that draw us to doubt, influenced by "evil spirits"). In each of our lives, we are impacted by the realities of good and evil. So, let's be sober and vigilant, and choose love.

1 Peter 5:5b–14
Psalm 89:2–3,6–7,16–17
Mark 16:15–20

Sunday April 26

• FOURTH SUNDAY OF EASTER •

[Jesus said,] "But whoever enters through the gate is the shepherd of the sheep.
The gatekeeper opens it for him, and the sheep hear his voice,
as the shepherd calls his own sheep by name and leads them out.
When he has driven out all his own,
he walks ahead of them, and the sheep follow him,
because they recognize his voice."

—JOHN 10:2–4

Like sheep, we grow and mature. Along the way, we develop our abilities to recognize whose voice is whose. We can recognize the tender touch of those who love us and hold us. On this holy Sabbath, let us rest in the trust that we are held by our Savior, the Good Shepherd. Let's listen closely to the tender, gentle voice of the caring Shepherd.

Acts 2:14a,36–41
Psalm 23:1–3a,3b–4,5,6 (1)
1 Peter 2:20b–25
John 10:1–10

"The Spirit told me to accompany them without discriminating."
—ACTS 11:12

Our faith tradition is rooted in indiscriminate accompaniment. We meet people where they are and accompany them as they search. When God is in charge of the agenda and the outcome, then we gain a freedom to simply walk alongside. We listen, encourage, and share what we can. As we offer kindness, we help others along their way. And we may be helped too.

Acts 11:1–18
Psalm 42:2–3; 43:3,4
John 10:11–18

Tuesday

APRIL 28

• ST. PETER CHANEL, PRIEST AND MARTYR •
ST. LOUIS GRIGNION DE MONTFORT, PRIEST •

[Jesus said,] "My sheep hear my voice;
I know them, and they follow me.
I give them eternal life, and they shall never perish.
No one can take them out of my hand."
—JOHN 10:27–28

Rev. Dr. Martin Luther King Jr.'s favorite song was "Take My Hand, Precious Lord," a hymn that expresses trust in the Good Shepherd, who guides us on. With our hand in his hand, we are held. We are helped onward. Today, let's turn to him and give him our worries, our needs. Let's give him our hands and let him lead us on.

Acts 11:19–26
Psalm 87:1b–3,4–5,6–7
John 10:22–30

Wednesday APRIL 29

• ST. CATHERINE OF SIENA, VIRGIN AND DOCTOR OF THE CHURCH •

May the nations be glad and exult
because you rule the peoples in equity;
the nations on the earth you guide.
—PSALM 67:5

No matter our nation of origin, we are children of God. The Creator of the entire cosmos is so personal and just that each of us is tended to with equity, care, and compassion. We can praise God for this greatness, and we can imitate our Holy Parent, too. Today is a good day to consider how we can contribute to a society that reflects the equity that comes from God.

Acts 12:24—13:5a
Psalm 67:2–3,5,6 and 8
John 12:44–50

Thursday APRIL 30

• ST. PIUS V, POPE •

When Jesus had washed the disciples' feet,
he said to them:
"Amen, amen, I say to you, no slave is greater
than his master
nor any messenger greater than the one
who sent him."
—JOHN 13:16

When he washed feet, Jesus bowed before others and demonstrated humility, showing us how to behave. So, let's find a way to be like Jesus today: to uplift another, to serve, and to gently tend to a need. If any of us is great, it's because God's grace allows us to serve in his name.

Acts 13:13–25
Psalm 89:2–3,21–22,25 and 27
John 13:16–20

Jesus said to his disciples:
"Do not let your hearts be troubled.
You have faith in God; have faith also in me.
In my Father's house there are many dwelling places.
If there were not,
would I have told you that I am going
to prepare a place for you?"
—JOHN 14:1–2

Since 1889, May 1 has been recognized as International Workers' Day: a time to celebrate the rights of workers and to advocate for more workers' rights, including fair pay and safety. In 1955, Pope Pius XII also marked May 1 as the Feast of St. Joseph the Worker. In Joseph, we see how labor is dignifying, and we are inspired to protect labor. *St. Joseph, patron saint of workers, pray for us. Amen.*

Acts 13:26–33
Psalm 2:6–7,8–9,10–11ab
John 14:1–6 or Matthew 13:54–58

Saturday
MAY 2

• ST. ATHANASIUS, BISHOP AND DOCTOR OF THE CHURCH •

The disciples were filled with joy and the Holy Spirit.
—ACTS 13:52

When a person is joyful, it can be an indicator of holiness—that they are full of the Holy Spirit. Listen for laughter. Notice who is beaming with exuberance. Pray today that the Holy Spirit enlivens you with gratitude, deep contentment, and zest for what's good. When you can, express the joy of knowing God's goodness. Show others the Holy Spirit's power.

Acts 13:44–52
Psalm 98:1,2–3ab,3cd–4
John 14:7–14

Sunday MAY 3

• FIFTH SUNDAY OF EASTER •

Beloved:
Come to him, a living stone, rejected by human beings
but chosen and precious in the sight of God,
and, like living stones,
let yourselves be built into a spiritual house
to be a holy priesthood to offer spiritual sacrifices
acceptable to God through Jesus Christ.
—1 PETER 2:4–5

Rejected by some yet accepted by God—and more than accepted—received, remade, encouraged, and called to bless and build God's reign. This happened to the Christians of the past, yes, but it is true for us, too: each one of us was named a priest at our Baptism, and we are commissioned to offer our lives for God's glory.

Acts 6:1–7
Psalm 33:1–2,4–5,18–19 (22)
1 Peter 2:4–9
John 14:1–12

"Men, why are you doing this?
We are of the same nature as you, human beings."
—ACTS 14:15

If we've ever experienced being worshiped as a hero because of achievement, fame, fortune, or success in our lives, Barnabas and Paul show us how to respond. If we do anything good or miraculous, it's because God is great and works through us. We are instruments of God's mercy. God is great and worthy of praise, not us. Let's allow God to work through us in amazing ways today.

Acts 14:5–18
Psalm 115:1–2,3–4,15–16
John 14:21–26

Jesus said to his disciples:
"Peace I leave with you; my peace I give to you.
Not as the world gives do I give it to you.
Do not let your hearts be troubled or afraid."
—JOHN 14:27

What is the peace of Christ, and how is it different from what the world gives? The peace of Christ is wholeness, oneness; peace is a contentment that outlasts any circumstance, a faith and confidence in the power of Christ's mercy that provides steadiness and strength even when we become troubled or frightened. This is all grace. We can pray and ask Jesus to help us know this peace.

Acts 14:19–28
Psalm 145:10–11,12–13ab,21
John 14:27–31a

[Jesus said,] "If you remain in me and my words remain in you,
ask for whatever you want and it will be done for you.
By this is my Father glorified,
that you bear much fruit and become my disciples."
—JOHN 15:7–8

When I was trained as a spiritual director, I found the image of nesting dolls to be helpful. Along with others in the cohort, I was taught to ask questions in a way that honored the reality of a person who is layered, who naturally moves from the superficial to the depths as they are prompted along with thoughtful questions. It could be true that our deepest self, our most true desires, are nestled in Christ.

Acts 15:1–6
Psalm 122:1–2,3–4ab,4cd–5
John 15:1–8

Sing to the LORD *a new song;*
sing to the LORD, *all you lands.*
Sing to the LORD; *bless his name.*
—PSALM 96:1–2

Today is a new day, a day you've never lived before. Perhaps each little act of love can be like a note in a symphony. Perhaps each loving choice can become part of a harmony, a song to give God praise. With every new chance to love, say *yes* to blessing God's name.

Acts 15:7–21
Psalm 96:1–2a,2b–3,10
John 15:9–11

[Jesus said,] "I have called you friends."
—JOHN 15:15

Consider the dynamics of friendship: trust, laughter, forgiveness, ease, and togetherness. True friends are happy to help, happy to listen, happy to do what they can to know the other person better. Friendship is the foundation of the church, of Christian community. And modern disciples have a simple mission: we develop Christ-centered friendships with one another. As we do, little by little, our bonds contribute to the strength of the church.

Acts 15:22–31
Psalm 57:8–9,10 and 12
John 15:12–17

Day after day the churches grew stronger in faith and increased in number.
—ACTS 16:5

The early Christians had such a zeal for their faith. Their passion for truth and love was contagious. Because of their witness, more people wanted to join their Christian communities. More people came to know belonging and joined the mission. Even today, Christians can expand their churches using the same formula. You can play a part.

Acts 16:1–10
Psalm 100:1b–2,3,5
John 15:18–21

Sunday MAY 10

• SIXTH SUNDAY OF EASTER •

Jesus said to his disciples:
"If you love me, you will keep my commandments."
—JOHN 14:15

A man I dated before entering the convent said he preferred to *show* me love, not talk about it. When he noticed what needed fixing in the house, he left and came back with supplies and made repairs. This is just one example of many countless gestures of kindness, care, affection, and generosity. I learned about love in those days. As a Franciscan Sister now, I aim to stay centered in an even deeper love—to show Christ I love him by how I say *yes* to his will.

Acts 8:5–8,14–17
Psalm 66:1–3,4–5,6–7,16,20
1 Peter 3:15–18
John 14:15–21

Monday
MAY 11

One of them, a woman named Lydia, a dealer
in purple cloth,
from the city of Thyatira, a worshiper of God,
listened,
and the Lord opened her heart to pay attention
to what Paul was saying.
After she and her household had been baptized,
she offered us an invitation,
"If you consider me a believer in the Lord,
come and stay at my home," and she prevailed on us.
—ACTS 16:14–15

Notice this pattern: the faithful businesswoman listened, committed herself to Christ, and immediately said *yes* to Christ's mission. Today, let's imitate this holy woman and generously offer warm hospitality to whomever God sends to us.

Acts 16:11–15
Psalm 149:1b–2,3–4,5–6a and 9b
John 15:26—16:4a

Tuesday
MAY 12

• ST. NEREUS AND ST. ACHILLEUS, MARTYRS • ST. PANCRAS, MARTYR •

[Jesus said,] "But I tell you the truth, it is better for you that I go."
—JOHN 16:7

We could cling to Jesus inside the safety of a church building. But we are Christians with a mission, and we are sent to serve—to encounter Jesus Christ who dwells in the world. We are empowered to represent Christ and serve those close to us and those who are on the fringes. We could pack sack lunches and offer them to people who live on the streets. We could fly to a foreign land and volunteer. Wherever we go, we encounter Christ.

Acts 16:22–34
Psalm 138:1–2ab,2cde–3,7c–8
John 16:5–11

Wednesday MAY 13

• OUR LADY OF FATIMA •

The God who made the world and all that is in it,
the Lord of heaven and earth,
does not dwell in sanctuaries made by human hands,
nor is he served by human hands
because he needs anything.
Rather it is he who gives to everyone life and
breath and everything.
—ACTS 17:24–25

Look around. Gaze at the beauty of God's creation. Notice the lines on your hands—hands made by God. Listen to your breath, to the air moving in and out. The air, your lungs, your heartbeat: all wonders made by God. Give thanks and honor God with your life.

Acts 17:15,22—18:1
Psalm 148:1–2,11–12,13,14
John 16:12–15

Thursday
MAY 14

• THE ASCENSION OF THE LORD •

May the eyes of your hearts be enlightened,
that you may know what is the hope that belongs
to his call,
what are the riches of glory
in his inheritance among the holy ones,
and what is the surpassing greatness of his power
for us who believe.
—EPHESIANS 1:18–19

Pause to pray:

God of hope, open my heart. I'm trying to listen to your call, deep inside my soul. I ask for your help to accept the graces you want to give me. May my reception to your will and grace transform me into a living witness of your glory and love. Amen.

Acts 1:1–11
Psalm 47:2–3,6–7,8–9 (6)
Ephesians 1:17–23
Matthew 28:16–20

Friday MAY 15

• ST. ISIDORE •

[Jesus said,] "So you also are now in anguish.
But I will see you again, and your hearts will rejoice,
and no one will take your joy away from you."
—JOHN 16:22

There are days when we feel the anguish of struggles. And there are days when hope becomes our strength. We are Easter people: we trust and believe that on the other side of suffering is great joy, a joy that only Christ can give.

Acts 18:9–18
Psalm 47:2–3,4–5,6–7
John 16:20–23

All you peoples, clap your hands;
shout to God with cries of gladness.
—PSALM 47:2

Our bodies are instruments to give God praise. We clap our hands. We lift our voices. We bow and kneel. We reach out and share God's mercy. With our bodies, we can show up and share. We can give our presence and adoration. May every gesture be an act of worship and an expression of love.

Acts 18:23–28
Psalm 47:2–3,8–9,10
John 16:23b–28

Beloved:
Rejoice to the extent that you share in the sufferings of Christ,
so that when his glory is revealed
you may also rejoice exultantly.
—1 PETER 4:13

As Christians, we don't try to avoid suffering. Rather, we surrender. We accept the pain of the Cross because we know the Cross is an expression of love. There's a paradoxical joy in knowing that Christ is with us in our sufferings, that we can commune with Christ in the worst of times. This is the mystery of God's love.

Acts 1:12–14
1 Peter 4:13–16
John 17:1–11a

When they heard this,
they were baptized in the name of the Lord Jesus.
—ACTS 19:5

When we speak, our words carry with them a great potential to impact others. The things we say could invite others to a deeper awareness, increase their imagination, or inform them. We don't know—and don't need to know—how our words will influence others and lead to great change, but God does. Let's be messengers of God.

Acts 19:1–8
Psalm 68:2–3ab,4–5acd,6–7ab
John 16:29–33

[Jesus prayed,] "I glorified you on earth by accomplishing the work that you gave me to do."
—JOHN 17:4

Here we have Jesus praying to God the Father with words that acknowledge he was a man with a mission, and the mission would continue far beyond his time on earth. We, too, are people on a mission: we are called to play a part in building up a church and society where peace and justice flourish. It can be tough, though, to know what our particular part is or where we should focus. St. Francis of Assisi was another man with a mission from God. Before he departed earth, he gave his brothers a blessing: "I have done what was mine to do. May God show you what is yours to do." May we pay attention well and respond to the mission God has for each of us.

Acts 20:17–27
Psalm 68:10–11,20–21
John 17:1–11a

Wednesday MAY 20

• ST. BERNARDINE OF SIENA, PRIEST •

And from your own group, men will come forward
perverting the truth
to draw the disciples away after them.
So be vigilant.
—ACTS 20:30–31

It's a harsh reality: tainted by sin and misinformation, people are tempted to pursue power. Sometimes this gets ugly, as folks distort the truth and cause confusion. When we feel uncertain about what's true, let us pray to be centered in Christ:

God of Truth, direct our attention to your love and mercy.
When the lure of drama or distortion tempts us,
steady our focus upon you and your grace.
Be our guide, our path, our way. Amen.

Acts 20:28–38
Psalm 68:29–30,33–35a,35bc–36ab
John 17:11b–19

Thursday MAY 21

• ST. CHRISTOPHER MAGALLANES, PRIEST, AND COMPANIONS, MARTYRS •

The following night the Lord stood by [Paul] and said, "Take courage."
—ACTS 23:11

Being on a faith journey requires taking risks. We venture toward mystery, enter into uncertainty, and embrace the unknown. It's no surprise many don't take their faith seriously. Who wants to give up control and be afraid? God, though, is trustworthy and encouraging. Love companions and guides us.

Acts 22:30; 23:6–11
Psalm 16:1–2a and 5,7–8,9–10,11
John 17:20–26

Peter was distressed that [Jesus] had said to him a third time,
"Do you love me?" and he said to him,
"Lord, you know everything; you know
that I love you."
Jesus said to him, "Feed my sheep."
—JOHN 21:17

We're called to love and act. Let's start with prayer: *God of love who knows the truth of who we are, who knows what's on our heart, your invitation to action is strong. Because of you, we turn to those who are hungry and small, small like sheep. We offer loaves and love, and little by little, love expands. Amen.*

Acts 25:13b–21
Psalm 103:1–2,11–12,19–20ab
John 21:15–19

[Jesus said to Peter,] "What concern is it of yours?
You follow me."
—JOHN 21:22

Every message from Christ offers an opportunity to be in conversation with God, to respond with love.

Jesus, these simple words you said to Peter are so clear and strong. You also communicate with me with simplicity and clarity. You speak your love and truth, and you remind me to focus on what's most important: following you. Thank you, Jesus. Amen.

Acts 28:16–20,30–31
Psalm 11:4,5 and 7
John 21:20–25

Sunday MAY 24

• PENTECOST SUNDAY •

There are different kinds of spiritual gifts
but the same Spirit;
there are different forms of service but the same Lord;
there are different workings but the same God
who produces all of them in everyone.
—1 CORINTHIANS 12:4–6

The Holy Spirit empowers us to serve. Some of us sing, some offer a listening ear, some serve food, and some are loving administrators. Our gifts are given to us by God so we can share them and give them back to God's mission. The Holy Spirit enlivens and empowers us to unite as one. Thank God that this is the way God designed it!

VIGIL:
Genesis 11:1–9 or Exodus 19:3–8a,16–20b
or Ezekiel 37:1–14 or Joel 3:1–5
Psalm 104:1–2,24,35,27–28 29,30
Romans 8:22–27
John 7:37–39

DAY:
Acts 2:1–11
Psalm 104:1,24,29–30,31,34
1 Corinthians 12:3b–7,12–13
John 20:19–23

Monday MAY 25

• THE BLESSED VIRGIN MARY, MOTHER OF THE CHURCH •

All these devoted themselves with one accord to prayer, together with some women, and Mary the mother of Jesus, and his brothers.
—ACTS 1:14

The early Christian community had Mary, the mother of Jesus, at its center. After his Ascension, I imagine that the disciples were grieving, longing for Jesus to be with him as he was before his Crucifixion. Maybe they were trying to understand all they experienced with Jesus and didn't know what to do. Mary and other women were there too, present to the sorrow and uncertainty. When we are grieving, we too can gather in prayer and be open to Mary's presence and love.

Genesis 3:9–15 or Acts 1:12–14
Psalm 87:1–2,3 and 5,6–7
John 19:25–34

Tuesday MAY 26

• ST. PHILIP NERI, PRIEST •

[Jesus told Peter,] "But many that are first will be last, and the last will be first."
—MARK 10:31

Imagine children all lined up, eagerly awaiting a chance to pick up their snack of juice and graham crackers. A likely routine in many schools. Then, imagine the chaos and emotion that erupts when the teacher says, "Now we're going to all turn around and face the other way. Those of you at the end of the line are now the first." So it is in the Kingdom of God: with Jesus as our teacher, so it is for us.

1 Peter 1:10–16
Psalm 98:1,2–3ab,3cd–4
Mark 10:28–31

• ST. AUGUSTINE OF CANTERBURY •

"But the word of the Lord remains forever."
—1 PETER 1:25

In our lifetime, we hear words whose meaning reverberates through the years: *I do. Goodbye. Retired. I promise*. Today we may hear words from God, everlasting words: *Love. Peace. Jesus Christ. Amen*. May the power of these words always reverberate in us.

1 Peter 1:18–25
Psalm 147:12–13,14–15,19–20
Mark 10:32–45

The LORD is good:
his kindness endures forever,
and his faithfulness, to all generations.
—PSALM 100:5

Today is another chance to notice God's goodness. Look around. Listen. What do you see around you that reveals God's goodness? Shelter, water, air, beauty, breath, body, heartbeat: although some things are fleeting, God's goodness remains.

1 Peter 2:2–5,9–12
Psalm 100:2,3,4,5
Mark 10:46–52

Friday
MAY 29

• ST. PAUL VI, POPE •

Above all, let your love for one another be intense,
because love covers a multitude of sins.
—1 PETER 4:8

With genuine love at our center, faith communities revolve around the power of mercy. There are those who were once lonely, lost, and persecuted, yet mercy has brought them belonging. There are those who were once hungry, sick, and unhoused, yet mercy provided for each need. Pope Francis has a book called *The Name of God Is Mercy*, just as a name for God is Love. With mercy and love as our center, we honor the holy among us; every person is a child of God.

1 Peter 4:7–13
Psalm 96:10,11–12,13
Mark 11:11–26

O God, you are my God whom I seek;
for you my flesh pines and my soul thirsts
like the earth, parched, lifeless and without water.
—PSALM 63:2

To be a spiritual seeker, to long for intimacy with Christ, can sometimes feel like the experience of being dehydrated. In our longings for water, we can become dizzy, weak, and disorientated. Yet living water is offered to us each day through community, Scripture, contemplation, and sacraments. Let's drink in the graces.

Jude 17,20b–25
Psalm 63:2,3–4,5–6
Mark 11:27–33

Sunday
MAY 31

• THE MOST HOLY TRINITY •

"The LORD, the LORD, a merciful and gracious God, slow to anger and rich in kindness and fidelity."
—EXODUS 34:6

In the Holy Trinity, we encounter the beauty of communal love. When love is outpoured to another, love expands and unity is formed. As we relate to the three unique persons of the Holy Trinity united in one God, may we learn how to receive and share God's love. Let's be channels of God's mercy and let love flow.

Exodus 34:4b–6,8–9
Daniel 3:52,53,54,55, (52b)
2 Corinthians 13:11–13
John 3:16–18

Monday

JUNE 1

• ST. JUSTIN, MARTYR •

Beloved:
May grace and peace be yours in abundance
through knowledge of God and of Jesus our Lord.
—2 PETER 1:2

Christians are commissioned to greet others with love and peace, and honor the inherent dignity of each person. The way we say *hello* reflects the graces we experience because we know Jesus Christ, because we are children of God. Offer a holy *hello*.

2 Peter 1:2–7
Psalm 91:1–2,14–15b,15c–16
Mark 12:1–12

Tuesday JUNE 2

• ST. MARCELLINUS AND ST. PETER, MARTYRS •

So Jesus said to them,
"Repay to Caesar what belongs to Caesar
and to God what belongs to God."
They were utterly amazed at him.
—MARK 12:17

Let's converse with Christ:

Jesus, I am amazed by you too! Maybe those who heard you respond to this question about the coin were amazed because you are clever and you were pointing away from the ways of the world to the ways of God. Perhaps the lesson here is to not possess too much—or to possess anything at all. Help me be free from holding on too tight to the things I like. Amen.

2 Peter 3:12–15a,17–18
Psalm 90:2,3–4,10,14 and 16
Mark 12:13–17

Wednesday JUNE 3

• ST. CHARLES LWANGA AND COMPANIONS, MARTYRS •

For God did not give us a spirit of cowardice but rather of power and love and self-control.
—2 TIMOTHY 1:7

Christians are known by their love, yes, but also by their courage. Because of the boldness of their faith and love, Christians venture to distant lands and share joy and compassion—a risk that requires courage. Because of the power God has given, Christians stand up for justice and human rights with hope that is brave and strong. How will you be courageous for Christ today?

2 Timothy 1:1–3,6–12
Psalm 123:1b–2ab,2cdef
Mark 12:18–27

[Jesus said,] "He is One and there is no other than he.
And to love him with all your heart,
with all your understanding,
with all your strength,
and to love your neighbor as yourself
is worth more than all burnt offerings and sacrifices."
—MARK 12:32–33

To give all we are to God—to choose to love—is an act of constant devotion. We show up and listen, share, serve, and hold others when they suffer. We stay steadfast in this mission because it matters, because it makes and remakes us. Through each act of loving God, neighbor, and self, we are made into the people God created us to be: his children, made in his image and showing the world that God is love.

2 Timothy 2:8–15
Psalm 25:4–5ab,8–9,10 and 14
Mark 12:28–34

Friday
JUNE 5

• ST. BONIFACE, BISHOP AND MARTYR •

All Scripture is inspired by God and is useful
for teaching,
for refutation, for correction,
and for training in righteousness,
so that one who belongs to God may be competent,
equipped for every good work.
—2 TIMOTHY 3:16–17

Apparently, one of the books most stolen from libraries is the Bible. As ironic as this may be, it reveals a truth: we ought not to take Scripture and its power for granted. We can honor the Word of God and all it reveals. We can savor Scripture and respect the love letter God has given us, reserving special spaces for the Bible in our home, in our day, and in our hearts. No matter how we choose to respect Scripture, let's make sure it energizes us to do good.

2 Timothy 3:10–17
Psalm 119:157,160,161,165,166,168
Mark 12:35–37

Saturday
JUNE 6

• ST. NORBERT, BISHOP •

Calling his disciples to himself, [Jesus] said to them,
"Amen, I say to you, this poor widow put in more
than all the other contributors to the treasury.
For they have all contributed from their surplus wealth,
but she, from her poverty, has contributed all she had,
her whole livelihood."
—MARK 12:43–44

Pour your heart out to Jesus, and perhaps your purse:
Dear Jesus, help me to be generous. Help me to give all that I am and all that I have to you and your mission. I want to follow the example of the saintly poor widow whom you uplifted. Open my eyes to see how I cling to things too tightly. Open my heart to the needs of others. Open my hands to give everything away. Amen.

2 Timothy 4:1–8
Psalm 71:8–9,14–15ab,16–17,22
Mark 12:38–44

• THE MOST HOLY BODY AND BLOOD OF CHRIST (CORPUS CHRISTI) •

Brothers and sisters:
The cup of blessing that we bless,
is it not a participation in the blood of Christ?
The bread that we break,
is it not a participation in the body of Christ?
—1 CORINTHIANS 10:16

Cups and bread—ordinary items made sacred by blessing and brokenness. The body of Christ is our body, and by our blessedness and brokenness, we are made one. Let us reverence and respect the sacredness of each person we encounter today: each body blessed, each body broken, each body becoming one with Christ.

Deuteronomy 8:2–3,14b–16a
Psalm 147:12–13,14–15,19–20 (12)
1 Corinthians 10:16–17
John 6:51–58

[Jesus said,] "Blessed are the clean of heart,
for they will see God."
—MATTHEW 5:8

Sometimes I think my eyes are failing me, until I realize that my glasses simply need to be cleaned. Once the smudges and specks of dirt are removed from my lenses, I gain a fresh perspective. I feel relieved. One place we can know and see God is in our hearts. If our hearts are distracted or cluttered with greed and selfishness, we may need to get out those cleaning rags—to go to the Sacrament of Reconciliation. With refreshed hearts, we may see God.

1 Kings 17:1–6
Psalm 121:1bc–2,3–4,5–6,7–8
Matthew 5:1–12

Tuesday JUNE 9

• ST. EPHREM, DEACON AND DOCTOR OF THE CHURCH •

Know that the LORD does wonders for his faithful one;
the LORD will hear me when I call upon him.
—PSALM 4:3

When the troubles and challenges of our lives make us feel as if we're being forced to sit out in the sun—to labor in the heat without sunscreen or relief—God is our shade, our rest, and our place of cooling. God guards and directs. God protects us from powers beyond our control. God is steady and does not abandon us.

1 Kings 17:7–16
Psalm 4:2–3,4–5,7b–8
Matthew 5:13–16

Wednesday

JUNE 10

[Elijah prayed,] "Answer me, LORD!
Answer me, that this people may know that you,
LORD, are God
and that you have brought them back to their senses."
The LORD's fire came down
and consumed the burnt offering, wood, stones,
and dust,
and it lapped up the water in the trench.
Seeing this, all the people fell prostrate and said,
The LORD is God! The LORD is God!"

—1 KINGS 18:37–39

As committed people of faith in a very competitive world, there are times when we might pray like Elijah, as if we want God to prove himself in grand and bold ways. Although the God of love may have won the battle with the ancient god, Baal, God seems to be in the business of expressing quiet mercy nowadays. God depends on us to show the world the fire of justice, the compassion of Christ. We are the ones who declare, "The LORD is God!"

1 Kings 18:20–39
Psalm 16:1b–2ab,4,5ab and 8,11
Matthew 5:17–19

Thursday JUNE 11

• ST. BARNABAS, APOSTLE •

[Jesus said,] "You have heard that it was said to your ancestors,
You shall not kill; and whoever kills will be liable
to judgment.
But I say to you, whoever is angry with his brother
will be liable to judgment."

—MATTHEW 5:21–22

All of us need food, water, belonging, mercy, shelter, and rest. At times we have all felt hungry, insecure, grumpy, joyful, overwhelmed, or tired. Fortunately, by God's good designs, we're not meant to go through life alone. We need community and compassion. We, too, have a chance to generously and compassionately listen and share. Through each gesture, we communicate who we are, and how we want others to treat us. We build bonds of communion.

Acts 11:21b–26; 13:1–3
Psalm 98:1,2–3ab,3cd–4,5–6
Matthew 5:20–26

Beloved, let us love one another,
because love is of God;
everyone who loves is begotten by God
and knows God.
Whoever is without love does not know God,
for God is love.
—1 JOHN 4:7–8

When God is abstract—when we picture God as too distant and separate from us—we may make faith tougher than it needs to be. We can wander and wallow in our questions and doubts. Who is God? How do I know if God is with me? These are normal human questions, and the word of God responds. Love is the answer, and God is love. To know God, love. To be close to God, love. To recognize God's presence and power, look for love. Love is the way.

Deuteronomy 7:6–11
Psalm 103:1–2,3–4,6–7,8,10
1 John 4:7–16
Matthew 11:25–30

Saturday

JUNE 13

• THE IMMACULATE HEART OF THE BLESSED VIRGIN MARY *
ST. ANTHONY OF PADUA, PRIEST AND DOCTOR OF THE CHURCH •

Elijah went over to him and threw his cloak over him.
Elisha left the oxen, ran after Elijah, and said,
"Please, let me kiss my father and mother goodbye,
and I will follow you."
—1 KINGS 19:19–20

Like Mary and the prophets who preceded her, we may have to let go of our attachments and agendas to respond to God's call. With surrender, trust, and courage, we can step into what is unknown.

2 Corinthians 5:14–21 or 1 Kings 19:19–21
Psalm 16:1b–2a and 5,7–8,9–10
Matthew 5:33–37 or Luke 2:41–51

Sunday JUNE 14

• ELEVENTH SUNDAY IN ORDINARY TIME •

"Therefore, if you hearken to my voice and keep my covenant,
you shall be my special possession,
dearer to me than all other people,
though all the earth is mine.
You shall be to me a kingdom of priests, a holy nation."
—EXODUS 19:5–6

The entire planet and all its people are precious and dear to God. As God's holy ones, we are commissioned to be as priests—people who bless and make offerings of our goods, our time, our talent, and ourselves. As we love, serve, bless, give, and witness, we unite beyond borders, cultures, and human constructs. God creates a new nation with one ruler—Jesus Christ.

Exodus 19:2–6a
Psalm 100:1–2,3,5 (3c)
Romans 5:6–11
Matthew 9:36—10:8

Monday JUNE 15

[Jesus said,] "Give to the one who asks of you,
and do not turn your back on one
who wants to borrow."
—MATTHEW 5:42

When Jesus challenges us to be more generous, we may need to begin with prayer:

Dear Jesus, do you want me to give everything away? To be reckless in my generosity? So many people are asking me for money, time, and "stuff." I feel dizzy when I consider the needs of the world, as if these needs are in tension with my desire to be prudent and wise. Maybe I don't need to fret or overthink your instructions. Maybe I simply need to be responsive and generous, to notice when my fists and my heart are clenched tight. Open my heart, Jesus, and help me to love. Amen.

1 Kings 21:1–16
Psalm 5:2–3ab,4b–6a,6b–7
Matthew 5:38–42

[Jesus said,] "For if you love those who love you,
what recompense will you have?
Do not the tax collectors do the same?
And if you greet your brothers and sisters only,
what is unusual about that?"
—MATTHEW 5:46–47

Whether we like it or not, Christians must stand out. The challenge is to be unusual and countercultural. In a world full of doubt, fear, and hate, we are bold with our faith, hope, and love. Our virtues demonstrate our communal identity and reveal who we truly are. So, yes, let's greet everyone today. Let's have courage to love whomever we encounter.

1 Kings 21:17–29
Psalm 51:3–4,5–6ab,11 and 16
Matthew 5:43–48

Wednesday

JUNE 17

You hide them in the shelter of your presence
from the plottings of men;
You screen them within your abode
from the strife of tongues.
—PSALM 31:21

The psalmist names God as shelter, as one who protects and shields. We may know this shelter to be a sturdy and expansive fortress, a modest home, or simply a warm blanket. Yet, by God's grace, we may never know the harm that God shields us from. For this grace, we give God thanks.

2 Kings 2:1,6–14
Psalm 31:20,21,24
Matthew 6:1–6,16–18

Thursday
JUNE 18

[Jesus taught,] "This is how you are to pray:
Our Father who art in heaven,
hallowed be thy name,
thy Kingdom come,
thy will be done,
on earth as it is in heaven.
Give us this day our daily bread;
and forgive us our trespasses,
as we forgive those who trespass against us;
and lead us not into temptation,
but deliver us from evil."
—MATTHEW 6:9–13

This prayer is likely very familiar to you, something you could recite without much thought. Yet each line is theologically rich, teaching us lessons about who God is, how we are called to be, and what is true, good, and just. Ponder the meaning of this prayer, and then find a new, fresh way to pray the words with greater intention.

Sirach 48:1–14
Psalm 97:1–2,3–4,5–6,7
Matthew 6:7–15

[Jesus said,] "For where your treasure is, there also will your heart be."
—MATTHEW 6:21

We are occupied: concerns fill our hearts and minds. Desires and ambitions motivate us to act. But what holds our heart, and where is our heart? It could be in our relationships, passions, or work. As we get in touch with our deepest desires, with what we most treasure, then we get in touch with the reality of our own hearts.

2 Kings 11:1–4,9–18,20
Psalm 132:11,12,13–14,17–18
Matthew 6:19–23

[Jesus said,] "Why are you anxious about clothes? Learn from the way the wild flowers grow."
—MATTHEW 6:28

Without extra effort, the dandelions stand tall and brighten the landscape, giving themselves away. The daisies dance. The violets cling to the sides of steep hills. The columbines reveal the intricacies of artistic design. Without extra effort, the wildflowers are authentic, steady, and free from anxiety. Jesus encourages us to learn from them, to notice how they grow.

2 Chronicles 24:17–25
Psalm 89:4–5,29–30,31–32,33–34
Matthew 6:24–34

Sunday
JUNE 21
• TWELFTH SUNDAY IN ORDINARY TIME •

Jesus said to the Twelve:
"Fear no one.
Nothing is concealed that will not be revealed,
nor secret that will not be known."
—MATTHEW 10:26

When we are centered in Christ, we can be brave. We can be truthful. Even when misinformation, confusion, manipulation, or doubt seeks to destroy unity and peace, we can depend on the mercy of God. God is always trustworthy. If we are guided by God alone, the grace of courage could come with ease.

Jeremiah 20:10–13
Psalm 69:8–10,14,17,33–35 (14c)
Romans 5:12–15
Matthew 10:26–33

Monday JUNE 22

• ST. PAULINUS OF NOLA, BISHOP *
ST. JOHN FISHER, BISHOP, AND ST. THOMAS MORE, MARTYRS •

Jesus said to his disciples:
"Stop judging, that you may not be judged.
For as you judge, so will you be judged,
and the measure with which you measure
will be measured out to you."
—MATTHEW 7:1–2

Christ's message here foreshadows what is found later in Scripture, in Galatians 6:7: "Make no mistake: God is not mocked, for a person will reap only what he sows." If you don't want others to judge you, don't judge them. If you want people to welcome you, welcome them. If you hope to be trusted, offer trust. If you want to gain friends, be a friend. If you want to feel grateful, be gracious. If you want to be forgiven, forgive others. For what we give, we receive.

2 Kings 17:5–8,13–15a,18
Psalm 60:3,4–5,12–13
Matthew 7:1–5

Tuesday

JUNE 23

"O LORD, *God of Israel, enthroned*
upon the cherubim!
You alone are God over all the kingdoms of the earth.
You have made the heavens and the earth.
Incline your ear, O LORD, *and listen!*
Open your eyes, O LORD, *and see!"*
—2 KINGS 19:15–16

Throughout the ages, humans have tried to make God look like them. We give God human features, such as ears and eyes. God, though, is holy mystery: infinite creativity, goodness, abundance, light, love, community, and mercy. St. Pope John Paul II even called God *Ocean* in his 1999 "Letter to Artists." Imagine, God the Ocean: deep, mysterious, life-giving, and expansive. This God is giant and amazing, and this God is near to you, aware of your heartbeat, alive in your breath. Consider how you are part of the holy mystery of God.

2 Kings 19:9b–11,14–21,31–35a,36
Psalm 48:2–3ab,3cd–4,10–11
Matthew 7:6,12–14

Wednesday JUNE 24

• THE NATIVITY OF ST. JOHN THE BAPTIST •

But the LORD answered me,
Say not, "I am too young."
To whomever I send you, you shall go;
whatever I command you, you shall speak.
—JEREMIAH 1:7

Some of us say that we're too young; others say we're too old, too tired, or too busy. It's so typical of us—so human of us—to come up with excuses and try to say *no*. But as the adage says, "God doesn't call the equipped; God equips the called." When God calls us to serve those in need, step out of our comfort zones, and speak up for justice, we better get out of God's way. We better say and do what we're made to do.

VIGIL:
Jeremiah 1:4–10
Psalm 71:1–2,3–4a,5–6ab,15ab and 17
1 Peter 1:8–12
Luke 1:5–17

DAY:
Isaiah 49:1–6
Psalm 139:1b–3,13–14ab,14c–15
Acts 13:22–26
Luke 1:57–66,80

Thursday JUNE 25

Remember not against us the iniquities of the past;
may your compassion quickly come to us,
for we are brought very low.
—PSALM 79:8

Imagine what today could be like if compassion came quickly. Maybe you could offer a dollar to the person in need. Perhaps you could carve out time to be a loving listener. Maybe a stranger will show up and give you the help you need. We don't have to worry about the burdens we bring along. With compassion, we are able to lift up the lowly. And we'll discover that we're uplifted too.

2 Kings 24:8–17
Psalm 79:1b–2,3–5,8,9
Matthew 7:21–29

When Jesus came down from the mountain,
great crowds followed him.
And then a leper approached, did him homage, and said,
"Lord, if you wish, you can make me clean."
[Jesus] stretched out his hand, touched him, and said,
"I will do it. Be made clean."
His leprosy was cleansed immediately.
—MATTHEW 8:1–3

The leper shows us a three-step process for prayer: express hopes and desires to God, trust in God's abilities, and surrender to God's will: "If you wish." Notice the needs around you—in your family, neighborhood, and church, and try this three-step process for prayer. As he did for the leper, maybe Jesus will hear you and say, "I will do it."

2 Kings 25:1–12
Psalm 137:1–2,3,4–5,6
Matthew 8:1–4

Saturday

JUNE 27

• ST. CYRIL OF ALEXANDRIA, BISHOP AND DOCTOR OF THE CHURCH •

Cry out to the Lord;
moan, O daughter Zion!
Let your tears flow like a torrent
day and night;
Let there be no respite for you,
no repose for your eyes.
—LAMENTATIONS 2:18

What a relief to know that our loving God is interested in all our thoughts and feelings and is with us through every emotion. Our prayers can be full of praise and thanksgiving, and we can literally groan and moan. We need to express our feelings in healthy ways for them to be transformed, and God is certainly the safest one to cry with. We can put all our sorrows on the altar like an offering.

Lamentations 2:2,10–14,18–19
Psalm 74:1b–2,3–5,6–7,20–21
Matthew 8:5–17

Sunday JUNE 28

• THIRTEENTH SUNDAY IN ORDINARY TIME •

[Jesus said,] "Whoever finds his life will lose it, and whoever loses his life for my sake will find it."
—MATTHEW 10:39

Like other religious traditions, Christianity is rich with paradoxes—two statements seem to be in contradiction, but together they become a deeper spiritual truth. These are the mighty mysteries of faith that we are invited to embrace. If we want to gain abundant life, then we give our lives away to Christ. We lose our lives, and after we lose it all, then we will discover life anew.

2 Kings 4:8–11,14–16a
Psalm 89:2–3,16–17,18–19 (2a)
Romans 6:3–4,8–11
Matthew 10:37–42

Monday JUNE 29

• ST. PETER AND ST. PAUL, APOSTLES •

I want you to know, brothers and sisters,
that the Gospel preached by me is not
of human origin.
For I did not receive it from a human being,
nor was I taught it,
but it came through a revelation of Jesus Christ.
—GALATIANS 1:11–12

The gospel mission of building up the Kingdom of God—helping all people to know the peace and justice that come from Jesus Christ—is not a mission of human origin. We are commissioned to do this work by God himself. Look for a chance to share the peace and justice that come from Jesus today.

VIGIL:
Acts 3:1–10
Psalm 19:2–3,4–5
Galatians 1:11–20
John 21:15–19

DAY:
Acts 12:1–11
Psalm 34:2–3,4–5,6–7,8–9
2 Timothy 4:6–8,17–18
Matthew 16:13–19

Tuesday
JUNE 30

• THE FIRST MARTYRS OF THE HOLY ROMAN CHURCH •

Then [Jesus] got up, rebuked the winds and the sea,
and there was great calm.
The men were amazed and said,
"What sort of man is this,
whom even the winds and the sea obey?"
—MATTHEW 8:26–27

Imagine how you would react if you were just getting to know Jesus, and then you saw the forces of nature and storms respond to his words right in front of you. Would you casually say, "Who is this guy?!" Or would you be frightened, disturbed, or confused? How might you react today if Jesus showed up and changed everything? Are you open to being amazed?

Amos 3:1–8; 4:11–12
Psalm 5:4b–6a,6b–7,8
Matthew 8:23–27

Hate evil and love good,
and let justice prevail at the gate.
—AMOS 5:15

When someone loves good, then much of their energy and attention are dedicated to expanding what is good. Today, choose to love good by looking for what is good around you. As you begin, notice the goodness of your breath, your body, and the freshness of a day with new opportunities in front of you. As the day unfolds, thank others for their kindness, help, and presence. As you notice and give thanks for the goodness, it could expand and flourish.

Amos 5:14–15,21–24
Psalm 50:7,8–9,10–11,12–13,16bc–17
Matthew 8:28–34

Thursday JULY 2

[Jesus] then said to the paralytic, "Rise, pick up your stretcher, and go home."
—MATTHEW 9:6

In a sense, each of us has experienced paralysis. For some, paralysis is physical. For others, our fears and sorrows stall our movements. Fortunately, Christ provides healing and transformation. No matter what has caused us to feel stuck and powerless, Jesus suggests certain steps: stand up, pick up what defined our former way of being, and move on.

Amos 7:10–17
Psalm 19:8,9,10,11
Matthew 9:1–8

Then [Jesus] said to Thomas, "Put your finger here and see my hands,
and bring your hand and put it into my side,
and do not be unbelieving, but believe."
—JOHN 20:27

For many of us, faith is an embodied experience. We grow in our faith because of what we touch, taste, smell, and eat. We have physical sensations when we feel the presence of the divine or encounter holiness. We worship with our bodies as we kneel, bow, genuflect, or sit still. And because we believe, we bring our bodies to the periphery, where the neglected need listening ears and gentle encouragement. May each gesture deepen our faith.

Ephesians 2:19–22
Psalm 117:1bc,2
John 20:24–29

Saturday JULY 4

• INDEPENDENCE DAY •

[Jesus said,] "People do not put new wine into old wineskins.
Otherwise the skins burst, the wine spills out,
and the skins are ruined.
Rather, they pour new wine into fresh wineskins,
and both are preserved."
—MATTHEW 9:17

As we change, so do the containers that hold us: homes, traditions, habits, and nations. It is worth taking an inventory of what's old and what's new and assess whether we are clinging to what was once comfortable and safe instead of considering how to create a new container for the newness that life offers. Newness can create freedom.

Amos 9:11–15
Psalm 85:9ab and 10,11–12,13–14
Matthew 9:14–17

Thus says the LORD:
Rejoice heartily, O daughter Zion,
shout for joy, O daughter Jerusalem!
—ZECHARIAH 9:9

Take a deep breath and draw to mind a time when you've felt joy. When your joy was so great you felt compelled to shout, and your heart felt as if it could burst with gladness. Rest in this memory and rejoice once again. Joyfulness is part of your mission today, and with God's grace, you can truly feel it now.

Zechariah 9:9–10
Psalm 145:1–2,8–9,10–11,13–14
Romans 8:9,11–13
Matthew 11:25–30

Monday JULY 6

• ST. MARIA GORETTI, VIRGIN AND MARTYR •

The LORD is gracious and merciful,
slow to anger and of great kindness.
—PSALM 145:8

It is a marvel, really. The God we love and adore, who created the mysterious universe and all its wonders, is kind. As God's children, we are made in God's likeness. We are designed to be kind, and we were created to share kindness with other creatures. So, we greet others with grins and offer compliments. We listen and offer care. Kindness may not be revolutionary or extraordinary, but it is absolutely necessary.

Hosea 2:16,17c–18,21–22
Psalm 145:2–3,4–5,6–7,8–9
Matthew 9:18–26

Tuesday JULY 7

Jesus went around to all the towns and villages,
teaching in their synagogues,
proclaiming the Gospel of the Kingdom,
and curing every disease and illness.
—MATTHEW 9:35

Tradition teaches us that Jesus is God made flesh and God is love, so here we have a demonstration that love is a verb more than a feeling. Jesus is busy, active, working hard, traveling, sharing, reaching outward, and expanding his circles of relationship and interaction. Love is open and expansive, inclusive and generous. We, too, are made to be busy with the activity of love.

Hosea 8:4–7,11–13
Psalm 115:3–4,5–6,7ab–8,9–10
Matthew 9:32–38

Wednesday JULY 8

"Sow for yourselves justice,
reap the fruit of piety;
break up for yourselves a new field,
for it is time to seek the LORD,
till he come and rain down justice upon you."
—HOSEA 10:12

For justice to flourish across all lands, God and God's people must work together. God is relying on our partnership—our participation—for every creature to flourish and be as God designed. For the little and vulnerable ones to be protected, for equity and fairness to be as common as air. This is our mission, and now is the time.

Hosea 10:1–3,7–8,12
Psalm 105:2–3,4–5,6–7
Matthew 10:1–7

Thursday JULY 9

• ST. AUGUSTINE ZHAO RONG, PRIEST, AND COMPANIONS, MARTYRS •

O shepherd of Israel, hearken.
From your throne upon the cherubim, shine forth.
Rouse your power.
—PSALM 80:2AC AND 3B

Jesus Christ proclaimed the reign of God: the peace and justice that were established through his birth, life, Death, and Resurrection. Part of our mission is to bridge the gap between the peace and justice that are fully known in heaven and what we know and experience in the here-and-now, among all creation. As we pray along with the psalmist who beckoned the Lord to "rouse your power," I wonder if this prayer might already be fulfilled: if the power for peace is here, among us, shining forth.

Hosea 11:1–4,8c–9
Psalm 80:2ac and 3b,15–16
Matthew 10:7–15

Jesus said to his Apostles:
"Behold, I am sending you like sheep
in the midst of wolves;
so be shrewd as serpents and as simple as doves."
—MATTHEW 10:16

Here Jesus acknowledges that the mission he gives his disciples is complex and challenging. It is worthwhile to pray for the graces of courage, cleverness, and wisdom so that we can proclaim the Good News. By God's grace and in God's love, we will be able to show up in the ways God needs us to.

Hosea 14:2–10
Psalm 51:3–4,8–9,12–13,14 and 17
Matthew 10:16–23

Then I heard the voice of the Lord saying,
"Whom shall I send? Who will go for us?"
"Here I am," I said; "send me!"
—ISAIAH 6:8

Once we say *yes* to God, we could be sent so many places.
Pray about where you could go.
To the margins of my comfort zone, send me Lord.
Beyond my despair and discouragement, send me Lord.
To the expansiveness of mercy and inclusion, send me Lord.
Beyond my fears and doubts, send me Lord.
Into deeper intimacy with you and your will, send me Lord. Amen.

Isaiah 6:1–8
Psalm 93:1ab,1cd–2,5
Matthew 10:24–33

Sunday JULY 12

• FIFTEENTH SUNDAY IN ORDINARY TIME •

My word shall not return to me void,
but shall do my will,
achieving the end for which I sent it.
—ISAIAH 55:11

Based in the Chicago area, the Sisters of the Living Word are a congregation of Catholic women religious who were founded in 1975. Their mission is something we can all get behind: to "reflect and affirm the Word in the world, the Word who continually frees the oppressed and gives new life" (Genevieve Shea, SLW, "Sisters of the Living Word 1975–1995 and Beyond").

Isaiah 55:10–11
Psalm 65:10,11,12–13,14
Romans 8:18–23
Matthew 13:1–23

Make justice your aim: redress the wronged,
hear the orphan's plea, defend the widow.
—ISAIAH 1:17

If we pay attention, each day offers an opportunity to love and serve: to listen to who is crying out for aid and advocacy, to let our hearts be moved with compassion. Each day offers a chance to love our neighbors. This day, reach outward and tend to the lonely and afflicted. Petition those in power so that the poor have what they need. Reorder the world to reflect the biblical justice where the needs of the oppressed and abandoned are centered over those with might and privilege. Make this your aim today.

Isaiah 1:10–17
Psalm 50:8–9,16bc–17,21 and 23
Matthew 10:34—11:1

Tuesday JULY 14

• ST. KATERI TEKAKWITHA, VIRGIN •

Take care you remain tranquil and do not fear;
let not your courage fail.
—ISAIAH 7:4

Christians are meant to develop many virtues as they mature: compassion, gentleness, kindness, and patience. You can add virtues to the litany by naming how you hope to grow, change, and better reflect Christ's light. As we pray for the graces we need to become the disciples God made us to be, let us not overlook the call to be courageous. Again and again we must step out of our comfort zones, take risks, and embrace uncertainties. With God's help, we become brave so that we can boldly share the good news that Christ reigns.

Isaiah 7:1–9
Psalm 48:2–3a,3b–4,5–6,7–8
Matthew 11:20–24

Wednesday JULY 15

• ST. BONAVENTURE, BISHOP AND DOCTOR OF THE CHURCH •

Jesus exclaimed:
"I give praise to you, Father, Lord of heaven and earth,
for although you have hidden these things
from the wise and the learned
you have revealed them to the childlike."
—MATTHEW 11:25

To know the truth, we need to listen to little ones. In many circumstances, those who are new and seemingly less powerful offer the freshest perspective. From their vantage and with their innocence, they see what others cannot. So, if you are a principal, ask the cook, custodian, or kindergartener for their ideas about how to improve the school. In your home, ask the youngest for their insights. We can learn much from those who may be overlooked.

Isaiah 10:5–7,13b–16
Psalm 94:5–6,7–8,9–10,14–15
Matthew 11:25–27

Thursday

July 16

• OUR LADY OF MOUNT CARMEL •

Jesus said:
"Come to me, all you who labor and are burdened,
and I will give you rest."
—MATTHEW 11:28

In the northern hemisphere, mid-July brings us to the time of year when many families go on vacation. We play on beaches or in parks and explore unfamiliar places. We choose to become intentional about rest, relaxation, and recreation because these practices re-create us, renew us, and restore our minds, bodies, and spirits. We were not made for labor alone. Resting in Christ is a holy activity.

Isaiah 26:7–9,11,16–19
Psalm 102:13–14ab and 15,16–18,19–21
Matthew 11:28–30

"If you knew what this meant, I desire mercy, not sacrifice, you would not have condemned these innocent men."
—MATTHEW 12:7

Each time we encounter another person, there's a chance we'll be met with judgment. They could be sizing us up, like it or not. Our biases and prejudices could be coloring our interactions. Yet each human person is a miracle and mystery, a child of God to honor and respect. Today, let's try to set aside standards, expectations, and outcomes and greet others with warmth and openness. We can let go of the temptation to condemn in favor of sharing mercy.

Isaiah 38:1–6,21–22,7–8
Isaiah 38:10,11,12abcd,16
Matthew 12:1–8

Saturday
JULY 18

• ST. CAMILLUS DE LELLIS, PRIEST •

Woe to those who plan iniquity,
and work out evil on their couches.
—MICAH 2:1

Tyrants and oppressors aren't ancient history. We may have encountered those who seem to enjoy inflicting suffering upon others in our communities, governments, and churches. We shudder to think of those who cause harm. Yet we're challenged to remember that we are also capable of and culpable for causing injury. Let's pray for societies that work toward greater healing.

Micah 2:1–5
Psalm 10:1–2,3–4,7–8,14
Matthew 12:14–21

Brothers and sisters:
The Spirit comes to the aid of our weakness;
for we do not know how to pray as we ought,
but the Spirit himself intercedes with
inexpressible groanings.
—ROMANS 8:26

There are times when we feel all we can offer to God is a heartfelt groan. So when prayer is difficult, we don't need to fret. The Spirit can come and pray through us. The Spirit offers us assistance and guidance. At those times, groaning is good enough.

Wisdom 12:13,16–19
Psalm 86:5–6,9–10,15–16 (5a)
Romans 8:26–27
Matthew 13:24–43

• ST. APOLLINARIS, BISHOP AND MARTYR •

You have been told, O man, what is good,
and what the LORD requires of you:
Only to do the right and to love goodness,
and to walk humbly with your God.
—MICAH 6:8

This Scripture verse offers some relief. Here we have a simple answer to a question that can cause a lot of torment—*What does God want of us?* God wants us to do what's right, to love what is good, and to humbly walk with God. How we show up to our tasks can reveal how we're doing at living this mission. Let us honor God with attitudes and actions that show how goodness is the love of our life.

Micah 6:1–4,6–8
Psalm 50:5–6,8–9,16bc–17,21 and 23
Matthew 12:38–42

Tuesday

JULY 21

• ST. LAWRENCE OF BRINDISI, PRIEST AND DOCTOR OF THE CHURCH •

[Jesus said,] "For whoever does the will of my heavenly Father is my brother, and sister, and mother."

—MATTHEW 12:50

Let's converse with Christ about the Gospel:

Jesus, I pray that I am doing the will of your heavenly Father. Jesus, I thank you for being my brother. I'm honored that you consider me part of your family. I ask for your grace so I can bring honor to our human family today, in the way that I love you, myself, and my neighbors. Amen.

Micah 7:14–15,18–20
Psalm 85:2–4,5–6,7–8
Matthew 12:46–50

Wednesday
JULY 22

• ST. MARY MAGDALENE •

So whoever is in Christ is a new creation: the old things have passed away; behold, new things have come.
—2 CORINTHIANS 5:17

It is refreshing to be made new and then notice how change brings us closer to Christ. Maybe we've become more gentle and generous, or we desire to spend more time in prayer. Maybe we've decided to volunteer instead of relaxing by ourselves. This is a grace, a chance to give thanks. Yet, when our habits and hearts change, we may need to notice what's ending as well. It's okay to grieve the old that has passed away and ritualize the endings. As we become new, let's allow our former ways to come to a graced conclusion.

Song of Songs 3:1–4b or
2 Corinthians 5:14–17
Psalm 63:2,3–34,5–6,8–9
John 20:1–2,11–18

• ST. BRIDGET OF SWEDEN, RELIGIOUS •

O LORD, your mercy reaches to heaven;
your faithfulness, to the clouds.
Your justice is like the mountains of God;
your judgments, like the mighty deep.
—PSALM 36:6

Like the universe, God's goodness is expansive and mysterious. We may not ever know or understand all of God's power, yet we can trust that God's mercy is poured over our questions and concerns.

Jeremiah 2:1–3,7–8,12–13
Psalm 36:6–7ab,8–9,10–11
Matthew 13:10–17

Friday
JULY 24

• ST. SHARBEL MAKHLŪF, PRIEST •

[Jesus said,] "The seed sown on rich soil
is the one who hears the word and understands it,
who indeed bears fruit and yields a hundred
or sixty or thirtyfold."
—MATTHEW 13:23

If we are to be like rich soil, ready to receive God's messages and be transformed, then it might be worth considering what acts like fertilizer to our souls. What habits and heartaches could go into the compost pit and be transformed? Perhaps acts of service, openness, and humility make us more receptive to God's grace. Maybe habits of study and retreat increase the likelihood that seeds will germinate and sprout new life.

Jeremiah 3:14–17
Jeremiah 31:10,11–12abcd,13
Matthew 13:18–23

Brothers and sisters:
We hold this treasure in earthen vessels,
that the surpassing power may be of God
and not from us.
—2 CORINTHIANS 4:7

Love speaks to you: I'm ready to provide all the power you need to live out my mission. When you are dedicated to the common good, I will provide the strength you need. Turn to the simple and ordinary, to the humblest of hearts, homes, and souls. I am eager to give you the riches of encouragement and hope.

2 Corinthians 4:7–15
Psalm 126:1bc–2ab,2cd–3,4–5,6
Matthew 20:20–28

Sunday
JULY 26

• SEVENTEENTH SUNDAY IN ORDINARY TIME •

"Give your servant, therefore, an understanding heart
to judge your people and to distinguish right
from wrong.
For who is able to govern this vast people of yours?"
—1 KINGS 3:9

There is likely to be a time in each of our lives when we are called to be a leader, when we'll need to act with some authority and wisdom. In such situations, this prayer could serve us well. Pray Solomon's prayer, and ask for the wisdom you need today.

1 Kings 3:5,7–12
Psalm 119:57,72,76–77,127–128,129–130 (97a)
Romans 8:28–30
Matthew 13:44–52

Monday

JULY 27

[Jesus said,] "The Kingdom of heaven is like yeast
that a woman took and mixed with three measures
of wheat flour
until the whole batch was leavened."
—MATTHEW 13:33

My grandmother's kitchen was often dusted with flour, the aroma of baking bread wafting through the house. It's where I learned how bread baking is ordinary holiness. Yeast, though, is powerful and life-giving, allowing simple grains to stretch and expand. And if there's anything off in the process—water too cold, for example—then the vulnerable yeast doesn't quite live up to its potential. This is the reality of building God's reign: the tiniest ones can be the mightiest, and as they are vulnerable, they are worthy of our care.

Jeremiah 13:1–11
Deuteronomy 32:18–19,20,21
Matthew 13:31–35

Tuesday JULY 28

[Jesus said,] "Then the righteous will shine like the sun in the Kingdom of their Father. Whoever has ears ought to hear."
—MATTHEW 13:43

I have a friend who likes to joke that she is organizing sainthood campaigns. She says she is keeping record of the holy virtues and activity of others, noticing when they are operating in ways that give God glory. Perhaps we could join my friend in paying attention to when others are glowing with love. Maybe we'll see and hear evidence of God's power in the lives of ordinary people.

Jeremiah 14:17–22
Psalm 79:8,9,11 and 13
Matthew 13:36–43

Wednesday

JULY 29

• ST. MARTHA, ST. MARY, AND ST. LAZARUS •

But I will sing of your strength
and revel at dawn in your mercy;
You have been my stronghold,
my refuge in the day of distress.
—PSALM 59:17

Consider how God has been your stronghold throughout your life. Remember the times that you felt protected, sheltered, helped, and uplifted. Reflect on these mercies, and write your own song of praise.

Jeremiah 15:10,16–21
Psalm 59:2–3,4,10–11,17,18
John 11:19–27 or Luke 10:38–42

Thursday JULY 30

• ST. PETER CHRYSOLOGUS, BISHOP AND DOCTOR OF THE CHURCH •

Indeed, like clay in the hand of the potter,
so are you in my hand, house of Israel.
—JEREMIAH 18:6

In order to become a pot, clay has to be pliable, receptive, and open to being changed. Every ordinary day, God holds and shapes us, reworking us with tender attention. Let us allow God to do with us what God wills.

Jeremiah 18:1–6
Psalm 146:1b–2,3–4,5–6ab
Matthew 13:47–53

Friday
JULY 31

• ST. IGNATIUS OF LOYOLA, PRIEST •

[Jesus] did not work many mighty deeds there because of their lack of faith.

—MATTHEW 13:58

Jesus wasn't always warmly received. Many doubted. Others critiqued. It seems that he didn't waste his energy on those who didn't believe that he could help them. Let's try to be among those who do rely on him, who trust him, and who are open to his help.

Jeremiah 26:1–9
Psalm 69:5,8–10,14
Matthew 13:54–58

Saturday

AUGUST 1

• ST. ALPHONSUS LIGUORI, BISHOP AND DOCTOR OF THE CHURCH •

[Jeremiah answered,] "Now, therefore, reform your ways and your deeds;
listen to the voice of the LORD your God.
—JEREMIAH 26:13

The loving voice of God speaks to you:
I beckon you to my heart, my friend, and invite you to leave your comfort zone.
I know that change can feel terrifying, but I assure you that I am holding you.
You can trust in me to tend to you. I will help you brightly beam with my love.
Listen with your heart. You can say *yes* to love.

Jeremiah 26:11–16,24
Psalm 69:15–16,30–31,33–34
Matthew 14:1–12

Sunday AUGUST 2

• EIGHTEENTH SUNDAY IN ORDINARY TIME •

[Jesus said to the disciples,] "There is no need for them to go away; give them some food yourselves."
—MATTHEW 14:16

Because of how our society is set up, we could think that being charitable means making referrals. When someone says they are hungry, we feel good directing them to the nearest food shelf or soup kitchen. Although in a different time and place, the apostles had a similar mindset, wanting to send people onward to eat. Jesus, though, challenged them, just as he challenges us. Let's give from our own abundance.

Isaiah 55:1–3
Psalm 145:8–9,15–16,17–18
Romans 8:35,37–39
Matthew 14:13–21

Monday

AUGUST 3

But now, listen to what I am about to state
in your hearing
and in the hearing of all the people.
—JEREMIAH 28:7

To listen deeply to God's message, you may not need a quiet heart. To hear what God has to say, you may not need a calm mind or a peaceful place. Instead of trying to tune out the noise, consider how to open wide your heart. With an open heart, perhaps you'll hear God speak to you through unexpected people. Perhaps you'll encounter a prophet, a messenger of truth and justice, in the most surprising place.

Jeremiah 28:1–17
Psalm 119:29,43,79,80,95,102
Matthew 14:22–36

Tuesday AUGUST 4

• ST. JOHN VIANNEY, PRIEST •

Then [Jesus's] disciples approached and said to him,
"Do you know that the Pharisees took offense
when they heard what you said?"
—MATTHEW 15:12

There was a time when I was told not to be so opinionated. I needed to be careful, I was told, or I might offend the wrong people. I heard the message but chose to not let my passion for the truth squelch my voice. Jesus shows us how to have courage and integrity. We might need to speak up, even if it disturbs people who are comfortable.

Jeremiah 30:1–2,2–15,18–22
Psalm 102:16–18,19–21,29 and 22–23
Matthew 15:1–2,10–14

Wednesday
AUGUST 5

• THE DEDICATION OF THE BASILICA OF ST. MARY MAJOR •

With age-old love I have loved you;
so I have kept my mercy toward you.
—JEREMIAH 31:3

God's love knows not the bounds of time. Before you were in your mother's womb, you were beloved. Your ancestors and your future descendants: deeply loved. God was with your neighbor and received them into the world with tender love when they were born. The strangers across the seas: cherished and cared for while they grew into adulthood. Notice and appreciate the love God has for every person.

Jeremiah 31:1–7
Jeremiah 31:10,11–12ab,13
Matthew 15:21–28

Thursday
AUGUST 6

• THE TRANSFIGURATION OF THE LORD •

But Jesus came and touched them, saying, "Rise, and do not be afraid."
—MATTHEW 17:7

Imagine the glory and drama of God's throne: fire, smoke, angels, and clouds. Imagine how you might respond if you were exposed to so much of God's transcendence and might in one moment. As you imagine, can you picture Christ's gentleness and encouragement? Even in the mighty moments, God offers us care and kindness.

Daniel 7:9–10,13–14
Psalm 97:1–2,5–6,9
2 Peter 1:16–19
Matthew 17:1–9

Friday

AUGUST 7

• ST. SIXTUS II, POPE, AND COMPANIONS, MARTYRS * ST. CAJETAN, PRIEST •

"Learn then that I, I alone, am God, and there is no god besides me."
—DEUTERONOMY 32:39

Put God first. Before you get out of bed, consider God's mercy. Before you reach for the cell phone, ask God to guide your speech and scrolling. Before you begin to eat, say, "Thank you, God." Before you begin to complain, say, "God, help me to be grateful and see the whole truth." Before you rest, praise God for another day.

Nahum 2:1,3; 3:1–3,6–7
Deuteronomy 32:35cd–36ab,39abcd,41
Matthew 16:24–28

Saturday

AUGUST 8

• ST. DOMINIC, PRIEST •

Then the LORD answered me and said:
Write down the vision
Clearly upon the tablets,
so that one can read it readily.
For the vision still has its time,
presses on to fulfillment, and will not disappoint.
—HABAKKUK 2:2–3

Today, on the Feast of St. Dominic, we give God thanks for the gift that St. Dominic was to the church and for the Dominicans throughout the world—the Order of Preachers—who are steadfast in their dedication to study and proclaim the truth. For them, and for the visionaries and truth tellers in every community, we pray. *Help us to heed your message, O God. Amen.*

Habakkuk 1:12—2:4
Psalm 9:8–9,10–11,12–13
Matthew 17:14–20

Sunday AUGUST 9

• NINETEENTH SUNDAY IN ORDINARY TIME •

He went up on the mountain by himself to pray.
—MATTHEW 14:23

Since the start of Christianity, holy ones have imitated Jesus's prayer life by going into solitude. We may not be comfortable being by ourselves, yet in the sacred space where we go to be alone with God, we could find peace and strength. Alone with Christ, we could be nourished and prepared to respond to the needs of a crowd.

1 Kings 19:9a,11–13a
Psalm 85:9,10,11–12,13–14 (8)
Romans 9:1–5
Matthew 14:22–33

Monday

AUGUST 10

• ST. LAWRENCE, DEACON AND MARTYR •

Jesus said to his disciples:
"Amen, amen, I say to you,
unless a grain of wheat falls to the ground and dies,
it remains just a grain of wheat;
but if it dies, it produces much fruit."
—JOHN 12:24

Contemplate what Christ is saying and consider what you might say in reply.

Dear Jesus, I love you, but I am not so sure I like the message here. Are you really saying that I must die in order for the offerings of my life to be fruitful? Perhaps you're trying to say that I need to abandon my desire to see the outcomes of efforts, to feel satisfied by my accomplishments. Or maybe you really want me to trust you and stay faithful, no matter the cost. Help me to understand the meaning of your message and how this applies to my life, Jesus. Amen.

2 Corinthians 9:6–10
Psalm 112:1–2,5–6,7–8,9
John 12:24–26

Tuesday
AUGUST 11

• ST. CLARE, VIRGIN •

Your decrees are my inheritance forever;
the joy of my heart they are.
—PSALM 119:111

St. Clare of Assisi (1194–1253), the cofounder of the Franciscan order, was dedicated in her pursuit of the privilege of poverty. Her heart burst in joy because of her desire to own nothing, to be defined by her love of Christ instead of by her possessions. She longed to pass this passion for poverty on to her spiritual descendants. Because she followed her heart, she became the first woman in church history to write a rule of life, and her impact is still felt in the church today. *St. Clare, pray for us. Amen.*

Ezekiel 2:8—3:4
Psalm 119:14,24,72,103,111,131
Matthew 18:1–5,10,12–14

Wednesday

AUGUST 12

• ST. JANE FRANCES DE CHANTAL, RELIGIOUS •

Jesus said to his disciples:
"If your brother sins against you,
go and tell him his fault between you and him alone."
—MATTHEW 18:15

Christ offers us a challenge: when someone has hurt you, try to resolve the conflict one-on-one. Aim to mend the relationship and protect the dignity of others. If others behave poorly, know that they are still worthy of honor and protection. All of us are God's children.

Ezekiel 9:1–7; 10:18–22
Psalm 113:1–2,3–4,5–6
Matthew 18:15–20

Thursday

AUGUST 13

• ST. PONTIAN, POPE, AND ST. HIPPOLYTUS, PRIEST, MARTYRS •

"The servant fell down, did him homage,
and said,
'Be patient with me, and I will pay you back in full.'
Moved with compassion the master of that servant
let him go and forgave him the loan."
—MATTHEW 18:26–27

Jesus tells a parable about a king who is moved with compassion to forgive a servant's loan but then that servant doesn't forgive the loan owed to him by a debtor. Most of us are guilty of inconsistencies; we can think we're worthy of special treatment, or ignore the needs of others for arbitrary reasons. The systems that Christ has established and that we are called to build up this day are systems of equity and justice. Let's be freed from prejudices today.

Ezekiel 12:1–12
Psalm 78:56–57,58–59,61–62
Matthew 18:21—19:1

• ST. MAXIMILIAN MARY KOLBE, PRIEST AND MARTYR •

I will remember the covenant I made.
—EZEKIEL 16:60

Love speaks to you:
My child, you may have turned away in the past and gone your own way, but I stayed with you. You may turn away from me again, but I will always be yours. I promised to love you through everything, no matter what choices you've made. I am true Love. I never break a promise. I am here, and I am always yours.

Ezekiel 16:1–15,60,63
Isaiah 12:2–3,4bcd,5–6
Matthew 19:3–12

Saturday

AUGUST 15

• THE ASSUMPTION OF THE BLESSED VIRGIN MARY •

[Mary sang,] "He has filled the hungry with good things, and the rich he has sent away empty."
—LUKE 1:53

Our blessed mother Mary sang the truth and knew its potential: God is the author of justice and mercy. God is the great equalizer, filling the hands of those without, while letting those whose hands are full receive no more. We each need something, and God distributes fairly. The witness of Mary impacts us all. We each can say *yes* to mercy.

VIGIL:
1 Chronicles 15:3–4,15–16; 16:1–2
Psalm 132:6–7,9–10,13–14
1 Corinthians 15:54b–57
Luke 11:27–28

DAY:
Revelation 11:19a; 12:1–6a,10ab
Psalm 45:10,11,12,16
1 Corinthians 15:20–27
Luke 1:39–56

Sunday
AUGUST 16

• TWENTIETH SUNDAY IN ORDINARY TIME •

For my house shall be called
a house of prayer for all peoples.
—ISAIAH 56:7

Consider the universality of faith: all are children of God, and all are invited to be part of his flock. Every church, a sanctuary—no one turned away. This is according to God's design. It could be good to get out of the way and open the doors wide.

Isaiah 56:1,6–7
Psalm 67:2–3,5,6,8 (4)
Romans 11:13–15,29–32
Matthew 15:21–28

Monday
AUGUST 17

A young man approached Jesus and said,
"Teacher, what good must I do to gain eternal life?"
—MATTHEW 19:16

We can admire the courage of the young man. He wanted to learn from Christ, and he was open to hearing what Christ could tell him. It's brave to be open to learning, to be receptive to challenges and new ideas. It demonstrates humility and a desire to grow in holiness. We can follow his example and turn to Jesus and ask our questions, too. We never know where the questions might take us.

Ezekiel 24:15–23
Deuteronomy 32:18–19,20,21
Matthew 19:16–22

Tuesday

AUGUST 18

Jesus said to his disciples:
"Amen, I say to you, it will be hard for one who is rich
to enter the Kingdom of heaven.
Again I say to you,
it is easier for a camel to pass through the eye
of a needle
than for one who is rich to enter
the Kingdom of God."
—MATTHEW 19:23–24

I've heard that the eye of the needles that camels passed through in Jesus's time were narrow passageways in a city wall, not a sewing needle like I imagined when I heard this Scripture as a puzzled child. There were times when camels and needles were as foreign to me as the concept of riches. But as I've aged, I've become more conscious of my wealth and privilege. I am not trying to figure out a puzzle anymore, and I'm praying that I am generous, faithful, and happy to redistribute and share wealth.

Ezekiel 28:1–10
Deuteronomy 32:26–27ab,27cd–28,30,35cd–36ab
Matthew 19:23–30

Wednesday

AUGUST 19

• ST. JOHN EUDES, PRIEST •

He guides me in right paths
for his name's sake.
—PSALM 23:3

Picture God as a guide. Do you sense that God is walking ahead of you on a treacherous path, scouting the danger and deciding the route? Or is God silent and gentle, redesigning the route as you move along? Or perhaps you know guides to be like lighthouses glowing across the waves. Consider how you know God as a guide, and how you respond.

Ezekiel 34:1–11
Psalm 23:1–3a,3b–4,5,6
Matthew 20:1–16

Thursday AUGUST 20

• ST. BERNARD, ABBOT AND DOCTOR OF THE CHURCH •

I will give you a new heart and place a new spirit within you,
taking from your bodies your stony hearts.
—EZEKIEL 36:26

Once again, Scripture reminds us that a major part of discipleship is transformation—*metanoia*, or in Christian theology, *conversion*. Whatever you call it, change and adaptation are part of what it means to be a person of faith. We ask God to help us develop and grow, and we trust that God will create us into vessels for the Spirit, better than we were before. *Change our hearts, O Christ. Amen.*

Ezekiel 36:23–28
Psalm 51:12–13,14–15,18–19
Matthew 22:1–14

[Jesus said,] "You shall love the Lord, your God,
with all your heart,
with all your soul, and with all your mind."
—MATTHEW 22:37

What does a life look like when a person loves God? Their heart and mind are occupied with the One they adore. Studying, service, worship, community building, and works of mercy are behaviors that show that the believer knows *love* is a verb, not a feeling. When God is number one above all material goods, comforts, and trends, a love-filled life is extraordinary.

Ezekiel 37:1–14
Psalm 107:2–3,4–5,6–7,8–9
Matthew 22:34–40

Saturday
AUGUST 22

• THE QUEENSHIP OF THE BLESSED VIRGIN MARY •

Kindness and truth shall meet;
justice and peace shall kiss.
—PSALM 85:11

These are virtues in a serene relationship. This psalm is more than quaint poetry. It's an invitation to mission. Today, we can imitate the holy ones we know and bundle kindness, truth, justice, and peace together into a strength that can help us navigate the worst of challenges. By God's grace and with strong virtues, we can reflect God's goodness.

Ezekiel 43:1–7ab
Psalm 85:9ab and 10,11–12,13–14
Matthew 23:1–12

Sunday
AUGUST 23

• TWENTY-FIRST SUNDAY IN ORDINARY TIME •

I will give thanks to you, O LORD, with all my heart.
—PSALM 138:1

There's a nearby opportunity to offer God wholehearted gratitude. We need not look far to find things to give thanks for. Let's start with our senses: what we see, hear, smell, taste, and touch. Feel the air move through your lungs. Consider your heart pumping blood. With every cell, every breath, every heartbeat—*thank you, God*.

Isaiah 22:19–23
Psalm 138:1–2,2–3,6,8 (8bc)
Romans 11:33–36
Matthew 16:13–20

Monday

AUGUST 24

• ST. BARTHOLOMEW, APOSTLE •

The wall of the city had twelve courses of stones
as its foundation,
on which were inscribed the twelve names
of the twelve Apostles of the Lamb.
—REVELATION 21:14

In our faith tradition and during our lifetimes, we inherit the legacies of those who have gone before us. Faithful martyrs and courageous leaders have built up the structures of what we now know. May we honor their foundations and be courageous to rebuild what could better respond to the needs of this time.

Revelation 21:9b–14
Psalm 145:10–11,12–13,17–18
John 1:45–51

Tuesday AUGUST 25

• ST. LOUIS, KING • ST. JOSEPH CALASANZ, PRIEST •

Jesus said:
"Woe to you, scribes and Pharisees, you hypocrites.
You pay tithes of mint and dill and cummin,
and have neglected the weightier things of the law:
judgment and mercy and fidelity."
—MATTHEW 23:23

Jesus's words may seem harsh. Jesus speaks truth, offering an uncomfortable challenge. Much is sacred in our faith tradition: places, artifacts, and rituals. If we get distracted and focus too much on what delights us—shiny metals, fancy lace, painted pillars, or prayerful gestures—then we are not focused on the One who creates the sacredness, the God of love who deserves all our devotion.

2 Thessalonians 2:1–3a,14–17
Psalm 96:10,11–12,13
Matthew 23:23–26

Wednesday

AUGUST 26

The LORD bless you from Zion:
may you see the prosperity of Jerusalem
all the days of your life.
—PSALM 128:5

We all have holy homes and sacred places where we belong. Some are actual places, such as a favorite church or tree, or in the arms of a beloved. Some may not be on a map. They could be in the quiet of our hearts. Go there now and unite with your God.

2 Thessalonians 3:6–10, 16–18
Psalm 128:1–2,4–5
Matthew 23:27–32

Thursday AUGUST 27

• ST. MONICA •

God is faithful,
and by him you were called to fellowship
with his Son, Jesus Christ our Lord.
—1 CORINTHIANS 1:9

Some may think that faith is about the absence of doubt and that faithfulness is dedication without question or challenge. God, though, remains with us even if we doubt or waver. We can give praise that certainty is not required to be part of God's family. We don't have to have strong or deep faith to belong to God. God is steadfast.

1 Corinthians 1:1–9
Psalm 145:2–3,4–5,6–7
Matthew 24:42–51

Friday
AUGUST 28

• ST. AUGUSTINE, BISHOP AND DOCTOR OF THE CHURCH •

The message of the cross is foolishness to those
who are perishing,
but to us who are being saved it is the power of God.
—1 CORINTHIANS 1:18

It is remarkable, really, that the Cross on which Jesus Christ died is a symbol of the triumphant power of God. Those who expect power and might to be glorious and wonderful certainly may consider the Cross to be foolish, or the reality that our Savior was tortured and killed, laughable. Jesus's surrender and selfless love *were* mighty, though. Besides, death doesn't have the last word. God's power and love change the most dire of circumstances.

1 Corinthians 1:17–25
Psalm 33:1–2,4–5,10–11
Matthew 25:1–13

Saturday AUGUST 29

• THE PASSION OF ST. JOHN THE BAPTIST •

Herod feared John, knowing him to be a righteous and holy man,
and kept him custody.
When he heard him speak he was very much perplexed,
yet he liked to listen to him.
—MARK 6:20

Today as we remember the gruesome way that St. John the Baptist was martyred, it's worth pausing to consider why he was considered a threat. He spoke the truth in a way that was attractive and fascinating, provoking thought and disturbance for the sake of God's reign. Maybe there's a way that you could do the same today. Maybe you could take a risk and speak the truth in a way that gives others pause.

1 Corinthians 1:26–31
Psalm 33:12–13,18–19,20–21
Mark 6:17–29

Sunday AUGUST 30

• TWENTY-SECOND SUNDAY IN ORDINARY TIME •

[Jesus said,] "What profit would there be for one to gain the whole world and forfeit his life?"
—MATTHEW 16:26

We could live to protect ourselves and our stuff, or we can imitate our brother Jesus, the one who offered freedom to others by giving up his comfort and his life. In simple ways, we can be generous by showing up to volunteer when we'd rather not; risking our own well-being to visit the sick; and by offering refreshment to the hungry and thirsty even if we're giving from our own limited supplies. As we give, we receive. We receive meaning, purpose, joy, and transformation.

Jeremiah 20:7–9
Psalm 63:2,3–4,5–6,8–9 (2b)
Romans 12:1–2
Matthew 16:21–27

Monday

AUGUST 31

I came to you in weakness and fear and much trembling,
and my message and my proclamation
were not with persuasive words of wisdom,
but with a demonstration of spirit and power,
so that your faith might rest not on human wisdom
but on the power of God.
—1 CORINTHIANS 2:4–5

Humans can be impressive: I think of the incredible performances, athletic talent, and inspiring leadership I've seen. In our faith communities, there are those who can preach, sing, teach, create, administer, and coordinate. Sometimes we're tempted to rally around charismatic personalities and give all our glory and praise to that person. But we have a chance to see that it is God's power and grace working through them. Let's give thanks for how God works through humans.

1 Corinthians 2:1–5
Psalm 119:97,98,99,100,101,102
Luke 4:16–30

Tuesday

SEPTEMBER 1

The Spirit scrutinizes everything,
even the depths of God.
—1 CORINTHIANS 2:10

We are children of God who are filled with the Spirit. This Scripture offers an invitation: we are called to know and explore God, holy mystery. Contemplation, centering prayer, meditation, study, creative acts, and spiritual practices may offer a glimmer of God's magnificence.

1 Corinthians 2:10b–16
Psalm 145:8–9,10–11,12–13ab,13cd–14
Luke 4:31–37

Wednesday

SEPTEMBER 2

At daybreak, Jesus left and went to a deserted place.
—LUKE 4:42

At the start or end of this day, we can imitate Christ: go to a deserted place, and savor the quiet and solitude. In the spaciousness, we may feel uncomfortable. We may be humbled by God's wonders. We may change into the person God has made us to be.

1 Corinthians 3:1–9
Psalm 33:12–13,14–15,20–21
Luke 4:38–44

Thursday

SEPTEMBER 3

• ST. GREGORY THE GREAT, POPE AND DOCTOR OF THE CHURCH •

Jesus said to Simon, "Do not be afraid;
from now on you will be catching men."
When they brought their boats to the shore,
they left everything and followed him.
—LUKE 5:10–11

Jesus spoke to Simon, and Jesus speaks to us. How might you speak to him?

Jesus, you invited the disciples to be brave and take risks. You are calling me to do the same, but I'm feeling a bit tentative. Can you strengthen my courage? Help me to be aware of what I am clinging to—what I struggle to let go of. I want to follow you, but I need you to coach me through the work of leaving things behind and going wherever you tell me to go. Help me, Jesus. Amen.

1 Corinthians 3:18–23
Psalm 24:1bc–2,3–4ab,5–6
Luke 5:10–11

Friday

SEPTEMBER 4

For [the Lord] will bring to light what is hidden in darkness
and will manifest the motives of our hearts,
and then everyone will receive praise from God.
—1 CORINTHIANS 4:5

A life of faith is an interior and exterior experience; a journey to encounter and know Christ in our hearts *and* out in the world. As we explore the holy mystery, we may doubt the truth or grow confused. We may not be sure if our motives are always right and pure. Do I continue to obey as a Christian because I love God and want to grow, or because the faith community keeps me comfortable? Whatever our motives may be, we can rely on Christ to reveal what's true.

1 Corinthians 4:1–5
Psalm 37:3–4,5–6,27–28,39–40
Luke 5:33–39

Saturday

SEPTEMBER 5

• ST. TERESA OF CALCUTTA, VIRGIN •

The LORD is just in all his ways
and holy in all his works.
The LORD is near to all who call upon him,
to all who call upon him in truth.
—PSALM 145:17–18

I've heard other Catholic Sisters talk about how their vows of poverty, obedience, and chastity are about radical availability. They want to be quickly available to serve whomever and however God calls them, unburdened by particular people, positions, or relationships. God, too, is radically available to us, present when we call out for help, ready to respond with justice and mercy. No matter our vocation, we can imitate the God we love.

1 Corinthians 4:6b–15
Psalm 145:17–18,19–20,21
Luke 6:1–5

Sunday

SEPTEMBER 6

• TWENTY-THIRD SUNDAY IN ORDINARY TIME •

Love does no evil to the neighbor;
hence, love is the fulfillment of the law.
—ROMANS 13:10

Christ speaks to you:

Dear friend, today is another day for you to open yourself to the power of love that surrounds you. I am pouring forth my love and offering it to you through the goodness of creation: the beauty of the trees, birdsong, clean water, and fresh air. Your body is healing and precious. Your heart is beautiful and beloved. You are made in love and for love, to be as generous and pure as the loving creation that you share life with. With me, flow with freedom like the trees, music, water, and wind.

Ezekiel 33:7–9
Psalm 95:1–2,6–7,8–9 (8)
Romans 13:8–10
Matthew 18:15–20

Monday

September 7

• LABOR DAY •

Your boasting is not appropriate.
Do you not know that a little yeast leavens
all the dough?
Clear out the old yeast, so that you may become
a fresh batch of dough,
inasmuch as you are unleavened.
—1 CORINTHIANS 5:6–7

There are times when we may feel satisfied and proud and are tempted to boast and brag about our accomplishments and virtues. I wonder if this happens because we don't know how to gently embrace our giftedness. I know that I squirm with discomfort when I hear compliments. I would rather deflect praise to God. We may feel a need to boast and judge, but here, the Bible says not to. God invites us to be tiny and small *and* as mighty as yeast. Pride and false humility decrease the power of potential, so let's clear out our vices.

1 Corinthians 5:1–8
Psalm 5:5–6,7,12
Luke 6:6–11

Tuesday

SEPTEMBER 8

• THE NATIVITY OF THE BLESSED VIRGIN MARY •

We know that all things work for good for those
who love God,
who are called according to his purpose.
—ROMANS 8:28

As baptized Christians, we each are called to serve God's purposes. Offer yourself to God.

Dear God, I may not be Mary, yet I wonder if there's a way that I could help incarnate your love in the world. I love you and want to do something good for you. Direct me today, as I discern how to do something good. I am all yours, and I am grateful to belong to you. Amen.

Micah 5:1–4a or Romans 8:28–30
Psalm 13:6ab,6c
Matthew 1:1–16,18–23

Wednesday

SEPTEMBER 9

• ST. PETER CLAVER, PRIEST •

Jesus said:
"Blessed are you who are poor,
for the Kingdom of God is yours.
Blessed are you who are now hungry,
for you will be satisfied."
—LUKE 6:20–21

We may have an inadequate supply of food and too few funds to buy groceries, or we may be too crushed by labor and schedules to pause for nourishment. If it is poverty that is keeping us hungry, Christ invites us to the banquet table. We see our neighbors build the reign of God around us as more people are fed, sheltered, honored, and respected. In the reign of God that Jesus established, all who crave justice will be nourished by the loving acts of others.

1 Corinthians 7:25–31
Psalm 45:11–12,14–15,16–17
Luke 6:20–26

Thursday

SEPTEMBER 10

Brothers and sisters:
Knowledge inflates with pride, but love builds up.
If anyone supposes he knows something,
he does not yet know as he ought to know.
But if one loves God, one is known by him.
—1 CORINTHIANS 8:1B–3

A young Jesuit was doing his philosophy homework, reading what medieval thinkers had to say about the nature of God. He felt challenged and confused. Were these ideas contradicting the belief system that brought him into religious life? Had he misunderstood the tenets of his faith for all these years? He vented to another Jesuit sitting nearby. The elder Jesuit listened kindly, thinking about how transformation requires humility. "The more you know, the more you realize that you don't know," he quipped. The new Jesuit was built up to love.

1 Corinthians 8:1b–7,11–13
Psalm 139:1b–3,13–14ab,23–24
Luke 6:27–38

Friday

SEPTEMBER 11

Even the sparrow finds a home,
and the swallow a nest
in which she puts her young—
Your altars, O LORD of hosts,
my king and my God!
—PSALM 84:4

Our God is the loving Creator of many—you, people in other countries, your annoying neighbor down the street, and swallows, elephants, kangaroos, rats, bees, and termites. Each creature is made and loved by the Great Designer, sheltered in compassion and care. Each earthly place can be a sanctuary for every member of God's holy family.

1 Corinthians 9:16–19,22b–27
Psalm 84:3,4,5–6,12
Luke 6:39–42

Saturday

SEPTEMBER 12

• THE MOST HOLY NAME OF MARY •

[Jesus said,] "From the fullness of the heart the mouth speaks."
—LUKE 6:45

It's so easy to fall into the traps of either-or thinking—dualism, as I've heard it called. But the mystics, saints, and wise elders encourage us to move out of those binaries that clump people into categories of "good" or "bad," "right" or "wrong." I probably label my own behaviors a hundred times a day. A beloved religious sister in my community has coached me into a deeper truth—every person is complex, including me. Allowing everyone the grace of *both/and* transforms mindsets and hearts. Perhaps, then, we can see ourselves and others from the fullness of the heart and can speak truth to one another in Christ's love.

1 Corinthians 10:14–22
Psalm 116:12–13,17–18
Luke 6:43–49

Sunday

SEPTEMBER 13

• TWENTY-FOURTH SUNDAY IN ORDINARY TIME •

Could anyone refuse mercy to another like himself,
can he seek pardon for his own sins?
—SIRACH 28:4

No matter the judgments and opinions that swirl through society, God remains merciful and ready to help. We are offered wholeness, belonging, freedom, and grace. We are freed through God's forgiveness and love. There's no hierarchy of sinfulness—all are deserving of grace and mercy. We have a chance to offer this grace to others. We are made to be merciful.

Sirach 27:30—28:7
Psalm 103:1–2,3–4,9–10,11–12 (8)
Romans 14:7–9
Matthew 18:21–35

Monday

SEPTEMBER 14

• THE EXALTATION OF THE HOLY CROSS •

God did not send his Son into the world
to condemn the world.
—JOHN 3:17

I am pretty convinced that the best stories contain good heroes. It's a bit mind-boggling to consider that my life story, your life story, and every human story is part of the story of God—part of the great story of salvation history. Our God came to be with us and to be one of us because that's the nature of love. The story of God's love is that it's liberating. The power of our stories is that we get to be liberators too. We can set people free by how we love.

Numbers 21:4b–9
Psalm 78:1bc–2,34–35,36–37,38
Philippians 2:6–11
John 3:13–17

Tuesday

SEPTEMBER 15

• OUR LADY OF SORROWS •

Standing by the cross of Jesus were his mother
and his mother's sister, Mary the wife Clopas,
and Mary Magdalene.
—JOHN 19:25

The mother of God stood by the Cross, staying close to her son as he suffered. As her children, we follow her example and find Christ in jails, hospitals, and shelters. We stand with those who are hurting, we hold them as they cry, and we accompany them in their oppression, heartache, and healing. We are with those who suffer, possibly lifting a little of the burden from their day. There are times, though, when the suffering breaks us down. The grief storms, a heaviness presses. We need care too. We can turn to Mary, who holds us as we struggle.

1 Corinthians 12:12–14,27–31a
Psalm 100:1b–2,3,4,5
John 19:25–27 or Luke 2:33–35

Wednesday

SEPTEMBER 16

• ST. CORNELIUS, POPE, AND ST. CYPRIAN, BISHOP, MARTYRS •

Love is patient, love is kind.
It is not jealous, love is not pompous,
it is not inflated, it is not rude,
it does not seek its own interests,
it is not quick-tempered, it does not brood over injury,
it does not rejoice over wrongdoing
but rejoices with the truth.
It bears all things, believes all things,
hopes all things, endures all things.
Love never fails.
—1 CORINTHIANS 13:4–8

God offers us a love letter today: a message and a lesson. We are challenged to notice how love is active and all around us. Who is acting with love?

1 Corinthians 12:31—13:13
Psalm 33:2–3,4–5,12 and 22
Luke 7:31–35

Thursday

SEPTEMBER 17

• ST. ROBERT BELLARMINE, BISHOP AND DOCTOR OF THE CHURCH
ST. HILDEGARD OF BINGEN, VIRGIN AND DOCTOR OF THE CHURCH •

Now there was a sinful woman in the city
who learned that he was at table in the house
of the Pharisee.
Bringing an alabaster flask of ointment,
she stood behind him at his feet weeping
and began to bathe his feet with her tears.
—LUKE 7:37–38

Imagine the scene: a talkative friend shows up in the woman's home. "He healed her!" the friend says. "You should hear him talk! He is a loving prophet! Oh, and he's right down the street, eating dinner in the Pharisee's house right now!" Her jar of precious ointment is in her hands, and she begins to run, drawn to love. She wordlessly falls at his dusty feet, sobbing with joy. She gently rubs the ointment into Jesus's callouses. He is strengthened and she is changed. This is the power of love.

1 Corinthians 15:1–11
Psalm 118:1b–2,16ab–17,28
Luke 7:36–50

Friday
SEPTEMBER 18

Brothers and sisters:
If Christ is preached as raised from the dead,
how can some among you say there is no
resurrection of the dead?
If there is no resurrection of the dead,
then neither has Christ been raised.
And if Christ has not been raised, then empty
too is our preaching;
empty, too, your faith.
—1 CORINTHIANS 15:12–14

Christ's Resurrection is a holy mystery of our faith, a testament that love has conquered the ultimate threat to our life—death itself. If we try to understand it in our minds, we may come to the limits of human logic and reason. Yet if we contemplate the meaning of it, our hearts and souls may be filled with assurance and hope. As our faith and love deepen, so, too, does our trust.

1 Corinthians 15:12–20
Psalm 17:1bcd,6–7,8b and 15
Luke 8:1–3

Saturday

SEPTEMBER 19

• ST. JANUARIUS, BISHOP AND MARTYR •

"But as for the seed that fell on rich soil,
they are the ones who, when they have heard
the word,
embrace it with a generous and good heart,
and bear fruit through perseverance."
—LUKE 8:15

Some of us start every day pondering the word of God. Perhaps you've prayed with this book every day all year, with hopes that you are like rich soil, embracing the Word with a generous heart. As we ponder, let us not forget to pray that the Word bears fruit in us: that we're kind in the face of cruelty, generous in the midst of scarcity, and hopeful in the most dire situations. No matter the setbacks or distractions, let us offer outreach and serve, so more can know Christ's peace.

1 Corinthians 15:35–37,42–49
Psalm 56:10c–12,13–14
Luke 8:4–15

Sunday

SEPTEMBER 20

• TWENTY-FIFTH SUNDAY IN ORDINARY TIME •

Seek the LORD while he may be found,
call him while he is near.
Let the scoundrel forsake his way,
and the wicked his thoughts;
let him turn to the LORD for mercy;
to our God, who is generous in forgiving.
—ISAIAH 55:6–7

The most effective servant leaders are those who were once burdened by sin and shame but have been changed and set free to help others. They have discovered that God's mercy is active and flowing: a grace that transforms and empowers. Unhindered by the past, they are freed to offer others compassion.

Isaiah 55:6–9
Psalm 145:2–3,8–9,17–18 (18a)
Philippians 1:20c–24,27a
Matthew 20:1–16a

Monday

SEPTEMBER 21

• ST. MATTHEW, APOSTLE AND EVANGELIST •

Brothers and sisters:
I, a prisoner for the Lord,
urge you live in a manner worthy of the call
you have received,
with all humility and gentleness, with patience,
bearing with one another through love,
striving to preserve the unity of the Spirit
through the bond of peace.
—EPHESIANS 4:1–3

Without community, we could not live out this biblical instruction. Let's reflect on who helps us along, who encourages us to live up to our commitments to Christ and stay steady in our devotion to love and peace. Whose life is an inspiring example? Perhaps we could express our love and appreciation for their help today. We need one another to know the bonds of peace.

Ephesians 4:1–7,11–13
Psalm 19:2–3,4–5
Matthew 9:9–13

Tuesday

SEPTEMBER 22

To do what is right and just
is more acceptable to the LORD than sacrifice.
—PROVERBS 21:3

Many athletes believe the adage "No pain, no gain." When it comes to building physical strength, the phrase may be apt. But when it comes to our religious devotion to living the gospel, love matters more than our sacrifice. Imitating the justice that Jesus demonstrates—uplifting the lowly, including the outcast—is most important. Doing what's right matters a lot.

Proverbs 21:1–6,10–13
Psalm 119:1,27,30,34,35,44
Luke 8:19–21

Wednesday

SEPTEMBER 23

• ST. PIO OF PIETRELCINA (PADRE PIO), PRIEST

[Jesus] said to them, "Take nothing for the journey, neither walking stick, nor sack, nor food, nor money, and let no one take a second tunic."

—LUKE 9:3

Just as what we wear makes a statement, what we carry also says a lot about us. Think of people carrying skateboards, books, guitars, shopping bags, or basketballs. In biblical times, there was a group of travelers called Cynics who carried walking sticks and knapsacks to show others that they were self-sufficient. Jesus's followers, though, were commissioned to be in solidarity with those they served—to be communal and interdependent. The Christian path is not about individualism or might but about a commitment to accompany others in mutual love.

Proverbs 30:5–9
Psalm 119:29,72,89,101,104,163
Luke 9:1–6

Thursday

SEPTEMBER 24

What has been, that will be;
what has been done, that will be done.
Nothing is new under the sun.
Even the thing of which we say, "See, this is new!"
has already existed in the ages that preceded us.
—ECCLESIASTES 1:9–10

During an era of rapidly changing technologies and ongoing societal shifts, this Scripture could seem outdated. The timeless truth in this passage, though, is that in every era there remains a steadiness because God's providence is in charge. In much of what's occurring, we're powerless and need to surrender to reality. We can see another timeless truth: "What is, is."

Ecclesiastes 1:2–11
Psalm 90:3–4,5–6,12–13,14 and 17bc
Luke 9:7–9

Friday

SEPTEMBER 25

Then [Jesus] said to them, "But who do you say that I am?"
Peter said in reply, "The Christ of God."
—LUKE 9:20

When I taught high school theology, I asked my students to contemplate the question above and consider what they'd say to Jesus in reply. Many students would list a lot of good yet predictable phrases: Savior, Messiah, or God. It was most interesting, though, when the students came up with words that revealed they had a relationship with Jesus, or hoped to develop one: friend, coach, buddy, and teammate. At each stage of our lives, it is worth considering who Jesus is for us.

Ecclesiastes 3:1–11
Psalm 144:1b and 2abc,3–4
Luke 9:18–22

Saturday

SEPTEMBER 26

• ST. COSMAS AND ST. DAMIAN, MARTYRS •

While they were all amazed at his every deed,
Jesus said to his disciples,
"Pay attention to what I am telling you.
The Son of Man is to be handed over to men."
—LUKE 9:43–44

When someone impresses us, it may be tough to take in the full picture of who they are. Jesus's followers were excited about his actions, but they didn't want to hear his whole message or accept the imminence of the Cross. We may have the same challenge—only wanting to see the glory and shying away from the suffering and cost of discipleship. With Christ, though, we can gain the strength to accept the whole picture.

Ecclesiastes 11:9—12:8
Psalm 90:3–4,5–6,12–13,14 and 17
Luke 9:43b–45

Sunday

SEPTEMBER 27

• TWENTY-SIXTH SUNDAY IN ORDINARY TIME •

Do nothing out of selfishness or out of vainglory;
rather, humbly regard others as more important
than yourselves,
each looking out not for his own interests,
but also for those of others.
—PHILIPPIANS 2:3–4

In the early stages of my formation as a Catholic sister, I clearly heard the message that religious life is a journey of downward mobility. Instead of climbing the ladder of achievement and power, we seek the humblest of positions that allow us to serve. Instead of seeking comfort and pleasure, we accept the anguish that is felt when one loves. Instead of being known and beloved for our greatness, we become smaller and more marginalized. This mission of being for others is the mission of all Christians.

Ezekiel 18:25–28
Psalm 25:4–5,6–7,8–9 (6a)
Philippians 2:1–11
Matthew 21:28–32

Monday

SEPTEMBER 28

• ST. WENCESLAUS, MARTYR • ST. LAWRENCE RUIZ AND COMPANIONS, MARTYRS •

[Jesus said,] "Whoever receives this child in my name receives me,
and whoever receives me receives the one
who sent me.
For the one who is least among all of you
is the one who is the greatest."
—LUKE 9:48

Today is another chance to listen and pay attention to the lesser ones that you encounter. Notice how the children gaze at the clouds and study the puddles. What message do they have to tell you? Let's revere the little ones for their greatness. Let's center the most vulnerable.

Job 1:6–22
Psalm 17:1bcd,2–3,6–7
Luke 9:46–50

Tuesday

SEPTEMBER 29

• ST. MICHAEL, ST. GABRIEL, AND ST. RAPHAEL, ARCHANGELS •

I will give thanks to you, O LORD, with all my heart,
for you have heard the words of my mouth;
in the presence of the angels I will sing your praise.
—PSALM 138:1–2

Here's a way to bring this psalm to life: remember God is with you and you are surrounded by angels. Make a list of what you're grateful for at this moment. Read the list out loud to God, speaking straight from your heart. Now, sing to God a hymn of praise.

Daniel 7:9–10, 13–14 or Revelation 12:7–12a
Psalm 138:1–2ab,2cde–3,4–5
John 1:47–51

Wednesday

SEPTEMBER 30

• ST. JEROME, PRIEST AND DOCTOR OF THE CHURCH •

Job answered his friends and said:
I know well that it is so;
but how can a man be justified before God?
Should one wish to contend with him,
he could not answer him once in a thousand times.
God is wise in heart and mighty in strength;
who has withstood him and remained unscathed?
—JOB 9:1–4

The book of Job is a story about enduring suffering, and it is part of the Wisdom literature of the Hebrew Bible. No matter how tough things become for Job, he never blames God for his suffering. Rather, he surrenders to God's mysterious power and accepts his reality while trusting in God's compassion. Perhaps we all can ponder why Job is considered wise.

Job 9:1–12,14–16
Psalm 88:10bc–11,12–13,14–15
Luke 9:57–62

Thursday
OCTOBER 1

• ST. THÉRÈSE OF THE CHILD JESUS, VIRGIN AND DOCTOR OF THE CHURCH •

[Jesus said,] "The harvest is abundant but the laborers are few;
so ask the master of the harvest
to send out laborers for his harvest."
—LUKE 10:2

All around, there's great abundance, *and* there's much work to do. Holy opportunity is everywhere. Each of us can consider what is needed and how we can contribute to building God's reign. How might I help share the harvest with others? How can I contribute to God's generous dream for all creation? Each time we say *yes* to our role, we help open space for others to know the nourishment that comes from God's table.

Job 19:21–27
Psalm 27:7–8a,8b–9abc,13–14
Luke 10:1–12

Friday OCTOBER 2

• THE HOLY GUARDIAN ANGELS •

O LORD, you have probed me and you know me;
you know when I sit and when I stand;
you understand my thoughts from afar.
My journeys and my rest you scrutinize,
with all my ways you are familiar.
—PSALM 139:1–3

God empowers angels to watch over us and protect us from danger. We may never see or sense these heavenly beings that are near, but they know us as God knows us. Along with the Holy Trinity and the communion of saints, angels provide shelter and invite us to grow in holiness. They're already in relationship with us. We can choose to be conscious of their presence.

Job 38:1,12–21; 40:3–5
Psalm 139:1–3,7–8,9–10,13–14ab
Matthew 18:1–5,10

Saturday

OCTOBER 3

The seventy-two disciples returned rejoicing
and said to Jesus,
"Lord, even the demons are subject to us
because of your name."
—LUKE 10:17

Demons may not have honored Jesus, but they understood who he was and knew the power of his name. Today, let's be on the lookout for ways to show Jesus that we not only know who he is and understand his power, but we also love him. Instead of lip service, let's serve the weak among us. Instead of good intentions, let's choose a simple, small act that honors Jesus. Instead of wordy prayers, let us dwell in the sanctity of power found in Jesus's name.

Job 42:1–3,5–6,12–17
Psalm 119:66,71,75,91,125,130
Luke 10:17–24

Sunday OCTOBER 4

• TWENTY-SEVENTH SUNDAY IN ORDINARY TIME •

Brothers and sisters:
Have no anxiety at all, but in everything,
by prayer and petition, with thanksgiving,
make your requests known to God.
Then the peace of God that surpasses all understanding
will guard your hearts and minds in Christ Jesus.
—PHILIPPIANS 4:6–7

Most people struggle with anxiety during their life. Whether it's because of a clinical diagnosis or stressful circumstances, we cannot always pray away the worries that weigh on our bodies and minds. Medical care may be necessary. Spiritual anxiety, though, is different. When our soul is taxed with concern and doubt, prayer is a pathway. As we surrender and receive God's grace, we may gain a sense of peace and come to know relief.

Isaiah 5:1–7
Psalm 80:9,12,13–14,15–16,19–20
Philippians 4:6–9
Matthew 21:33–43

Monday

OCTOBER 5

• ST. FAUSTINA KOWALSKA, VIRGIN •
BLESSED FRANCIS XAVIER SEELOS, PRIEST •

[Jesus asked,] "Which of these three, in your opinion, was neighbor to the robbers' victim?" [The man] answered, "The one who treated him with mercy." Jesus said to him, "Go and do likewise."

—LUKE 10:36–37

The parable of the Good Samaritan offers insight into the human tendency to make excuses. When we're busy or feel important, we don't want to take responsibility for our neighbor. We can throw up our hands and say, "Not my job." Jesus, though, has empowered each of us to be instruments of mercy and compassion. Caring for others—even strangers—is likely to be the most important work we ever do. When it comes to this mission, we need not stall.

Galatians 1:6–12
Psalm 111:1b–2,7–8,9 and 10c
Luke 10:25–37

Tuesday

OCTOBER 6

• ST. BRUNO, PRIEST * BL. MARIE ROSE DUROCHER, VIRGIN •

The Lord said to her in reply,
"Martha, Martha, you are anxious
and worried about many things.
There is need of only one thing.
Mary has chosen the better part
and it will not be taken from her."
—LUKE 10:41–42

Isn't it true that we develop opinions about how things are meant to go? Our preferences can so easily turn into judgment and resentment. Here's good news: Jesus offers freedom and joy. Maybe what made Mary's choice "better" was that she was content and totally focused on Jesus. Jesus invites us to offer fidelity and love.

Galatians 1:13–24
Psalm 139:1b–3,13–14ab,14c–15
Luke 10:38–42

Wednesday OCTOBER 7

• OUR LADY OF THE ROSARY •

Jesus was praying in a certain place,
and when he had finished,
one of his disciples said to him,
"Lord, teach us to pray just as John taught
his disciples."
—LUKE 11:1

In the Ignatian tradition, we come to know Jesus as a friend with a lively personality to whom we can turn to ask questions. We can get to know his moods and behaviors. We can be like the disciples and talk to Jesus about everything. We may even ask, "How do you want me to pray today, Jesus?" Then we might be surprised by what we hear: go to Mass, try the Rosary, care for your neighbor, write a letter, say an Our Father, or be still. Let's be ready to respond.

Galatians 2:1–2,7–14
Psalm 117:1bc,2
Luke 11:1–4

Thursday

OCTOBER 8

[Jesus said,] "And I tell you, ask and you will receive;
seek and you will find;
knock and the door will be opened to you."
—LUKE 11:9

Jesus may want us to understand that he is present and available, ready to respond to our requests. This would have made sense to his followers in first-century Palestine. The challenge is that we live in a different time and culture. Today, we are influenced by a transactional economy where we expect to receive a service or response if we pay the right price. Some bring this mindset to church, expecting that they'll always get something out of the experience. The point, though, is noticing the openings offered to us and acting with gratitude and love.

Galatians 3:1–5
Luke 1:69–70,71–72,73–75
Luke 11:5–13

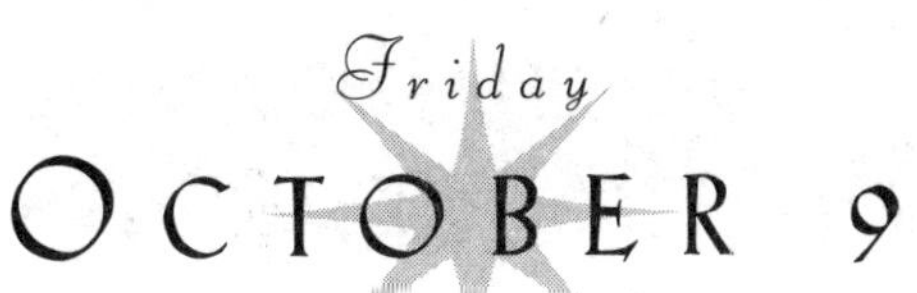

Friday OCTOBER 9

• ST. DENIS, BISHOP, AND COMPANIONS, MARTYRS
ST. JOHN LEONARDI, PRIEST •

[Jesus said,] "Every kingdom divided against itself
will be laid waste
and house will fall against house."
—LUKE 11:17

Let us pray that we each help build unity where there is division:

Holy God, you warn about the dangers of division, and I am disturbed, too. I am burdened by the polarities and strife I see in relationships, communities, families, the church, and the nation. I feel pressured to pick a side and take a stand. But then you show me the holiness of unity: you are three persons united as One. I invite you to show me how I can foster unity where it's needed. Help me to love like you. Amen.

Galatians 3:7–14
Psalm 111:1b–2,3–4,5–6
Luke 11:15–26

Saturday

OCTOBER 10

For through faith you are all children of God
in Christ Jesus.
For all of you who were baptized into Christ
have clothed yourselves with Christ.
There is neither Jew nor Greek,
there is neither slave nor free person,
there is not male and female;
for you are all one in Christ Jesus.
—GALATIANS 3:26–28

The human mind loves to create binaries in order to make sense of mystery: male vs. female, bright vs. dark, old vs. young. But God invites us to move beyond the binaries. God is ready to liberate us from the traps of categories. God is infinite. In Christ, we see beyond the limits of the human mind and know that "all are one."

Galatians 3:22–29
Psalm 105:2–3,4–5,6–7
Luke 11:27–28

Sunday OCTOBER 11

• TWENTY-EIGHTH SUNDAY IN ORDINARY TIME •

The Lord GOD will wipe away
the tears from every face;
the reproach of his people he will remove
from the whole earth; for the LORD has spoken.
—ISAIAH 25:8

God's love is like a fountain, constantly overflowing and readily available. We may be so busy or burdened that it can be difficult for us to notice and receive the graces of God's love, to feel how the ripples of the fountain offer us comfort and strength. Today is another Sabbath, a chance to carve out some contemplative time to bathe in God's love.

Isaiah 25:6–10a
Psalm 23:1–3a,3b–4,5,6 (6cd)
Philippians 4:12–14,19–20
Matthew 22:1–14

Monday

OCTOBER 12

From the rising to the setting of the sun
is the name of the LORD to be praised.
—PSALM 113:3

In time zones throughout the world, monks and nuns gather at the start and end of each day to sing praise to God. They praise God on our behalf, and they hold our intentions in prayer. We can thank God for their hidden and quiet vocation that sustains our church and its mission. From wherever we are, let us also give God praise.

Galatians 4:22–24,26–27,31—5:1
Psalm 113:1b–2,3–4,5a and 6–7
Luke 11:29–32

Tuesday

OCTOBER 13

For freedom Christ set us free;
so stand firm and do not submit again
to the yoke of slavery.
—GALATIANS 5:1

Here's another paradox of our faith: when we're longing for a feeling of freedom, we are *already* free. This may seem like a contradiction, but it is a deep truth and mystery. When we feel pressure or doubt, God's goodness is bigger than our feelings or thoughts. So let's trust and rejoice and behave like the free people we are: unhindered by the setbacks and ready to laugh at the traps in our path. God's goodness is more than we can fathom.

Galatians 5:1–6
Psalm 119:41,43,44,45,47,48
Luke 11:37–41

Wednesday

OCTOBER 14

• ST. CALLISTUS I, POPE AND MARTYR •

[Jesus said,] "Woe to you Pharisees!
You love the seat of honor in synagogues
and greetings in marketplaces.
Woe to you!
You are like unseen graves over which people
unknowingly walk."
—LUKE 11:43–44

I do it too: I place too much value on things that are unimportant. When I become rigid in my rules and expectations, my consciousness can become cluttered, preventing me from being compassionate, welcoming, and accepting. Thank God I have a chance to reset my habits and let go of my judgments so I can focus on what matters most: loving Jesus with a pure heart.

Galatians 5:18–25
Psalm 1:1–2,3,4 and 6
Luke 11:42–46

Thursday

OCTOBER 15

• ST. TERESA OF JESUS, VIRGIN AND DOCTOR OF THE CHURCH •

In love he destined us for adoption to himself through
Jesus Christ,
in accord with the favor of his will,
for the praise of the glory of his grace
that he granted us in the beloved.
—EPHESIANS 1:5–6

With Jesus Christ as our brother, we are members of the family of God. As you encounter others today, you could pray in gratitude for a chance to meet another brother or sister in Christ. Notice your common identity as children of God.

Ephesians 1:1–10
Psalm 98:1,2–3ab,3cd–4,5–6
Luke 11:47–54

Friday

OCTOBER 16

• ST. HEDWIG, RELIGIOUS • ST. MARGARET MARY ALACOQUE, VIRGIN •

[Jesus said,] "There is nothing concealed that will not be revealed,
nor secret that will not be known.
Therefore whatever you have said in the darkness
will be heard in the light,
and what you have whispered behind closed doors
will be proclaimed on the housetops."
—LUKE 12:2–3

Sometimes we'd rather not know the whole truth. We'd rather take in reality from the perspective that pleases us, that confirms our biases and ideals. I'd rather not entertain the idea that people avoid telling me when my hair is a mess because they are trying to be polite. Like it or not, though, the truth will eventually come out: I'll eventually overhear someone admit their opinion about my look. Then I'll have a real challenge in front of me: dealing with the truth.

Ephesians 1:11–14
Psalm 33:1–2,4–5,12–13
Luke 12:1–7

Saturday

OCTOBER 17

• ST. IGNATIUS OF ANTIOCH, BISHOP AND MARTYR •

[Jesus said,] "When they take you before synagogues and before rulers and authorities,
do not worry about how or what your defense will be
or about what you are to say.
For the Holy Spirit will teach you at that moment
what you should say."

—LUKE 12:11–12

The Gospels were written a generation or two after Jesus walked on earth, when it was risky to be a Christian. Hence, Scripture is full of messages that encourage the faithful to be brave and trust the Holy Spirit's guidance. In our time, it may not be as dangerous to live our faith, yet we may find ourselves in some holy trouble. When the time comes, let's not plan our speeches. Let's aim to be in communion with Christ. Then we'll have everything we need.

Ephesians 1:15–23
Psalm 8:2–3ab,4–5,6–7
Luke 12:8–12

Sunday
October 18

• TWENTY-NINTH SUNDAY IN ORDINARY TIME •

[Jesus said,] "Then repay to Caesar what belongs to Caesar and to God what belongs to God."
—MATTHEW 22:21

Let's respond to Jesus:

Jesus, like us, I know you lived in a complex time in history; a time when politics and oppressive systems created challenges for regular people. It seems you knew how to navigate your time with ease and grace, to discern how to participate yet be unattached. What do you want me to understand about how I can navigate the time that I am in? I'm listening, Jesus. Amen.

Isaiah 45:1,4–6
Psalm 96:1,4–5,7–8,9–10 (7b)
1 Thessalonians 1:1–5b
Matthew 22:15–21

Monday OCTOBER 19

• ST. JOHN DE BRÉBEUF AND ST. ISAAC JOGUES, PRIESTS, AND COMPANIONS, MARTYRS •

Then [Jesus] said to the crowd,
"Take care to guard against all greed,
for though one may be rich,
one's life does not consist of possessions."
—LUKE 12:15

When St. Ignatius of Loyola wrote "The First Principle and Foundation," he declared that we are loved by God and all things are gifts that are meant to help us return love to God. St. Ignatius writes, "We should not fix our desires on health or sickness, wealth or poverty, success or failure, a long life or a short one." Put another way, if we are clinging to stuff, a state of being, or an outcome, then we are distracted from remembering that everything is a gift and we are made to love.

Ephesians 2:1–10
Psalm 100:1b–2,3,4ab,4c–5
Luke 12:13–21

Tuesday OCTOBER 20

• ST. PAUL OF THE CROSS, PRIEST •

He came and preached peace to you who were far off
and peace to those who were near,
for through him we both have access
in one Spirit to the Father.

So then you are no longer strangers and sojourners,
but you are fellow citizens with the holy ones
and members of the household of God.
—EPHESIANS 2:17–19

The Prince of Peace speaks:
You may feel lost or lonely, yet I am with you. You may feel uncertain where you fit, yet you play a role. You may wonder about your purpose, yet I am calling you. Listen to me and look around. See the gifts I've given you. Each person is a gift, too. I love you and am glad you're family.

Ephesians 2:12–22
Psalm 85:9ab–10,11–12,13–14
Luke 12:35–38

Wednesday

OCTOBER 21

Jesus said to his disciples:
"Be sure of this:
if the master of the house had known the hour
when the thief was coming,
he would not have let his house be broken into.
You also must be prepared,
for at an hour you do not expect,
the Son of Man will come."
—LUKE 12:39–40

An aspect of following Jesus that we might overlook is the element of surprise. Our God is a God of surprises, often upsetting the status quo and inviting us to expand our imaginations. It's important to stay open and flexible; we never know when God might show up.

Ephesians 3:2–12
Isaiah 12:2–3,4bcd,5–6
Luke 12:39–48

Thursday OCTOBER 22

• ST. JOHN PAUL II, POPE •

Jesus said to his disciples:
"I have come to set the earth on fire,
and how I wish it were already blazing!"
—LUKE 12:49

"The love of God is a fire," the monk told a group gathered at the retreat house. The devout retreatants listened intently and filled their notebooks, nodding their heads. "The love of God purifies like fire does," the monk said. "It shows us what is most true. Jesus set the world ablaze with love. Do you see it?"

Ephesians 3:14–21
Psalm 33:1–2,4–5,11–12,18–19
Luke 12:49–53

Friday

OCTOBER 23

• ST. JOHN OF CAPISTRANO, PRIEST •

[Jesus said,] "You hypocrites!
You know how to interpret the appearance of the earth and the sky;
why do you not know how to interpret the present time?"
—LUKE 12:56

In the Catholic tradition, the faithful are challenged to interpret the "signs of the times." We are studious and active. We work to stay socially conscious and engage in analysis and theological reflection to understand how world problems connect to our faith. We are contemplative and prayerful. And we are discerning, asking Christ how to better love God and God's people. In short, we try to pay attention and respond in love.

Ephesians 4:1–6
Psalm 24:1–2,3–4ab,5–6
Luke 12:54–59

Saturday
OCTOBER 24

• ST. ANTHONY MARY CLARET, BISHOP •

I rejoiced because they said to me,
"We will go up to the house of the LORD."
—PSALM 122:1

Remember when you were a child, and you were excited to see people? You may have jumped and squealed with joy. Maybe you were giddy when your friends came over to play. God is always reaching out to you, pouring out love and dazzling you with beauty and goodness. God invites you to come out and play. Today is a great day to offer God an enthusiastic response to the invitation in front of you.

Ephesians 4:7–16
Psalm 122:1–2,3–4ab,4cd–5
Luke 13:1–9

Sunday

October 25

• THIRTIETH SUNDAY IN ORDINARY TIME •

I love you, O LORD, my strength,
O LORD, my rock, my fortress, my deliverer.
My God, my rock of refuge,
my shield, the horn of my salvation, my stronghold!
—PSALM 18:2–3

Most of us don't hang out in fortresses nowadays, but we probably know something about what it's like to feel under attack. I'll spare us a litany of reasons we may be overwhelmed; perhaps you want to have a conversation with Jesus about what is taxing you today. And then, you can imagine God as a strong fortress that protects you. Whenever you need a break, God is ready to offer you refuge and boost you back up for the challenge ahead.

Exodus 22:20–26
Psalm 18:2–3,3–4,47,51 (2)
1 Thessalonians 1:5c–10
Matthew 22:34–40

Monday

October 26

Be imitators of God, as beloved children,
and live in love,
as Christ loved us and handed himself over for us
as a sacrificial offering to God for a fragrant aroma.
—EPHESIANS 5:1–2

When I was a teacher, my students' personalities made sense once I met their parents. *Oh, this is why they're the way they are!* Like it or not, each of us inherited characteristics from our parents. We reveal who our parents are through our personalities. The God of love is also our Parent. Our actions and attitudes can show that we are God's children. Maybe when others notice us being bold or loving, they might think, *Oh, this is why they're the way they are, they're a Christian!*

Ephesians 4:32—5:8
Psalm 1:1–2,3,4 and 6
Luke 13:10–17

Tuesday

OCTOBER 27

Again [Jesus] said, "To what shall I compare the
Kingdom of God?
It is like yeast that a woman took
and mixed in with three measures of wheat flour
until the whole batch of dough was leavened."
—LUKE 13:20–21

Let us think about the ingredients that make up bread and imagine how we are part of the baking process.

Lord, in your hands I feel so small, like a speck of flour or yeast. You are the divine Baker who holds me and joins me with others, mixing and stirring so life expands, community is built, and people are fed. Help me to be content with playing my small and valuable part, even though I may never fully understand what I am helping to create. I am at your service, Lord. Amen.

Ephesians 5:21–33
Psalm 128:1–2,3,4–5
Luke 13:18–21

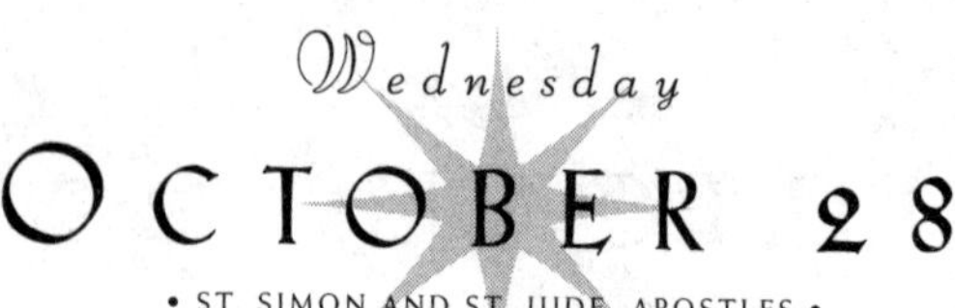

Wednesday OCTOBER 28

• ST. SIMON AND ST. JUDE, APOSTLES •

Brothers and sisters:
You are not longer strangers and sojourners,
but you are fellow citizens with the holy ones
and members of the household of God.
—EPHESIANS 2:19

This Scripture offers us a chance to reflect: As "members of the household of God," how are we meant to behave? What are we called to focus on? Let's make sure that non-Christians can tell that we're working on unity and holiness. Let's be a healthy and holy family, one that honors the head of our household, Christ.

Ephesians 2:19–22
Psalm 19:2–3,4–5
Luke 6:12–16

Thursday

OCTOBER 29

"Jerusalem, Jerusalem,
you who kill the prophets and stone those sent to you,
how many times I yearned to gather your
children together
as a hen gathers her brood under her wings,
but you were unwilling!"
—LUKE 13:34

Here Jesus shows us more of who he is. We can imagine a mother hen, gentle and strong, who fiercely protects her vulnerable chicks by holding them close. When we are weak or lost, Jesus offers us care and community. When we are distracted, Jesus reaches out to us. Jesus recenters us in his love and holds us under his wings.

Ephesians 6:10–20
Psalm 144:1b,2,9–10
Luke 13:31–35

Friday

October 30

I give thanks to my God at every remembrance of you,
praying always with joy in my every prayer
for all of you,
because of your partnership for the Gospel
from the first day until now.
—PHILIPPIANS 1:3–5

If you were St. Paul, writing this letter today, to whom would you want to convey this message of gratitude? Today could be a good day to give thanks. Give thanks to those who support us in our journey of faith. Thanks be to God for those who help us deepen our life of faith.

Philippians 1:1–11
Psalm 111:1–2,3–4,5–6
Luke 14:1–6

Saturday

OCTOBER 31

[Jesus said,] "For everyone who exalts himself will be humbled, but the one who humbles himself will be exalted."

—LUKE 14:11

Today, many people throughout the United States will celebrate Halloween, a holiday with holy roots. Celtic Catholics understood the veil between heaven and Earth to be thin this time of year. And many Catholics practice *memento mori* year-round—remembering our death. On Halloween we remember that Christ conquered the threat of death through his Resurrection. So, we taunt and tease wickedness by saying we can't be spooked. Evil doesn't frighten us because we are children of God, and we know it is sacred that we all will enter into the humus of earth someday.

Philippians 1:18b–26
Psalm 42:2,3,5cdef
Luke 14:1,7–11

[Jesus said,] "Rejoice and be glad,
for your reward will be great in heaven."
—MATTHEW 5:12

Today, on the Feast of All Saints, we pray with hope that we, too, are on a journey toward sainthood. Today, we celebrate the communion of saints: ordinary and extraordinary holy ones, not unlike us, who intercede for us and are glad in heaven. They are our family. For them we give thanks.

Revelation 7:2–4,9–14
Psalm 24:1b–2,3–4ab,5–6
1 John 3:1–3
Matthew 5:1–12a

Monday

NOVEMBER 2

• THE COMMEMORATION OF ALL THE FAITHFUL DEPARTED (ALL SOULS' DAY) •

The souls of the just are in the hand of God,
and no torment shall touch them.
They seemed, in the view of the foolish, to be dead;
and their passing away was thought an affliction
and their going forth from us, utter destruction.
But they are in peace.
—WISDOM 3:1–3

I have a friend who says, "Grief is a monster." I agree. When our loved ones die and depart from us in this life, the separation is tumultuous. Intense emotions come and go in waves, and we feel powerless in the pain. Doubt and big questions can weigh us down. Yet we can gain strength in knowing that God is with us and assures us that our loved ones rest in peace.

Wisdom 3:1–9
Romans 5:5–11 or 6:3–9
John 6:37–40
Other readings may be selected.

Tuesday

NOVEMBER 3

• ST. MARTIN DE PORRES, RELIGIOUS •

Have among yourselves the same attitude
that is also yours in Christ Jesus,
Who, though he was in the form of God,
did not regard equality with God
something to be grasped.
—PHILIPPIANS 2:5–6

For much of my life, I've admired other people, sometimes teetering toward idolizing them. I know firsthand that looking up to others can cause me to strive to be something that I'm not. If I am looking up to Jesus, though, I see a model for humility and downward mobility. I see an invitation to offer God the best of my true self.

Philippians 2:5–11
Psalm 22:26b–27,28–30ab,30e,31–32
Luke 14:15–24

Wednesday

NOVEMBER 4

• ST. CHARLES BORROMEO, BISHOP •

[Jesus said,] "Which of you wishing to construct a tower
does not first sit down and calculate the cost
to see if there is enough for its completion?
Otherwise, after laying the foundation
and finding himself unable to finish the work
the onlookers should laugh at him and say,
'This one began to build but did not have
the resources to finish.'"

—LUKE 14:28–30

When we make ourselves available for God's service, we can easily stall on starting our mission. With God's grace, we can make it through.

God, I don't want folks to laugh at me for my foolish choices. I want to think things through: to plan with wisdom and prudence. I want to be resourceful instead of impulsive. May I be ready to make the right investments of my time, talent, and funds. With your grace, may I finish the projects that give you glory and help others to know your love. Amen.

Philippians 2:12–18
Psalm 27:1,4,13–14
Luke 14:25–33

Thursday

NOVEMBER 5

The tax collectors and sinners were all drawing near
to listen to Jesus,
but the Pharisees and scribes began to complain,
saying,
"This man welcomes sinners and eats with them."
—LUKE 15:1–2

When an effective leader challenges the status quo—as Jesus did—people swarm near them and respond in different ways. Some desire to hear a message; they lean in and listen close, hoping to learn and act. Others remain guarded and cautious. And then there are critics who are loud and harsh with their complaints. When it comes to responding to Christ, which one are you?

Philippians 3:3–8a
Psalm 105:2–3,4–5,6–7
Luke 15:1–10

Friday

NOVEMBER 6

But our citizenship is in heaven,
and from it we also await a savior, the Lord
Jesus Christ.
—PHILIPPIANS 3:20

We live in a time in human history when human-constructed borders, citizenship, and procedures have great impact. These structures have so much power over our travel, work, study, and residency that we may be tempted to forget that our true belonging is not to a system but to God. As citizens of heaven, let us ensure that love is the rule that directs our lives.

Philippians 3:17—4:1
Psalm 122:1–2,3–4ab,4cd–5
Luke 16:1–8

Saturday

NOVEMBER 7

[Jesus said,] "The person who is trustworthy in very small matters
is also trustworthy in great ones;
and the person who is dishonest in very small matters
is also dishonest in great ones."

—LUKE 16:10

Without the bonds of trust, we fall apart. And by "we," I mean relationships, structures, communities, parishes, and families. When we demonstrate to others that we are trustworthy, we show them that we value the relationship and peace felt between us. When we step up and do what we say—help out at the event, sign the petition—we are building a world centered on love.

Philippians 4:10–19
Psalm 112:1b–2,5–6,8a and 9
Luke 16:9–15

Sunday

NOVEMBER 8

• THIRTY-SECOND SUNDAY IN ORDINARY TIME •

Jesus told his disciples this parable:
"The kingdom of heaven will be like ten virgins
who took their lamps and went out to meet
the bridegroom."
—MATTHEW 25:1

In the telling of this parable, Jesus is encouraging us to be people of virtue—full of wisdom, prudence, dedication, and devotion. We can imagine the scene: there's darkness and glowing light; there are those who are calm and those who are fearful; there's preparation and waiting; there's hope, faith, and love. The Kingdom of Heaven contains multitudes, indeed. So let us open our eyes to see how near it is.

Wisdom 6:12–16
Psalm 63:2,3–4,5–6,7–8 (2b)
1 Thessalonians 4:13–18
Matthew 25:1–13

Monday

NOVEMBER 9

• THE DEDICATION OF THE LATERAN BASILICA •

Do you not know that you are the temple of God,
and that the Spirit of God dwells in you?
If anyone destroys God's temple,
God will destroy that person;
for the temple of God, which you are, is holy.
—1 CORINTHIANS 3:16–17

Sacred spaces are a central part of our faith tradition. In Rome, before we had St. Peter's Basilica in Vatican City, the center of the Roman Catholic Church was the St. John Lateran Basilica. The former palace was converted into a church by Constantine once Christianity was legalized in the Roman empire. The basilica is considered the Mother Church of all churches throughout the world. On this church's feast, let's meditate on our connection to the global church and its complex history. Let us notice the abundance of sacred spaces that nourish our spiritual lives, especially our own bodies, where God meets us and holds us close.

Ezekiel 47:1–2,8–9,12
Psalm 46:2–3,5–6,8–9
1 Corinthians 3:9c–11,16–17
John 2:13–22

Tuesday

NOVEMBER 10

• ST. LEO THE GREAT, POPE AND DOCTOR OF THE CHURCH •

[Jesus said,] "When you have done all you have been commanded, say,
'We are unprofitable servants;
we have done what we were obliged to do.'"
—LUKE 17:10

Like Jesus and the apostles, we are situated in a society that is concerned with social status. And for many, status is connected to achievement. The church that Christ established isn't a meritocracy. We are part of a community. And, in community, we each are meant to give and receive, serve and be served. Pope Francis tells us that "greatness and success in God's eyes are measured differently: they are measured by service. Not on what someone has, but on what someone gives." Let's be great in God's eyes, not society's. Let's love and serve.

Titus 2:1–8,11–14
Psalm 37:3–4,18 and 23,27 and 29
Luke 17:7–10

Wednesday

NOVEMBER 11

• ST. MARTIN OF TOURS, BISHOP •

But when the kindness and generous love
of God our savior appeared,
not because of any righteous deeds we had done
but because of his mercy,
he saved us through the bath of rebirth
and renewal by the Holy Spirit,
whom he richly poured out on us
through Jesus Christ our savior.
—TITUS 3:4–6

At every Mass, we beg God for mercy. *Lord, have mercy. Christ, have mercy*. At the same time, we are already swimming in mercy, bathing in it, refreshed and readied to wash others in its power. And with the Holy Spirit's help and God's grace abundantly present, we have a chance to share that mercy with others; to bring others to the banquet of love. Let's crowd around the table.

Titus 3:1–7
Psalm 23:1b–3a,3bc–4,5,6
Luke 17:11–19

Thursday

NOVEMBER 12

• ST. JOSAPHAT, BISHOP AND MARTYR •

The LORD secures justice for the oppressed,
gives food to the hungry.
The LORD sets captives free.
—PSALM 146:7

As people of God, we are guaranteed to experience change for the better. We move from captivity to freedom, from hunger to nourishment. Yet even if the change is good for us or what we hope for, we may resist what's new. We don't feel ready for what's unknown and unpredictable. Let's pray to be open to the changes God offers. With God's grace, we can find adapting easier.

Philemon 7–20
Psalm 146:7,8–9a,9bc–10
Luke 17:20–25

Friday
NOVEMBER 13

• ST. FRANCES XAVIER CABRINI, VIRGIN •

For this is love, that we walk according to his commandments.
—2 JOHN 6

Mother Frances Xavier Cabrini moved from Italy to New York in 1889 along with six other religious sisters to care for Italian immigrants. With determination and few resources, she and her sisters took great risks and did everything they could to serve God's people. Grounded in a passion for justice and Christ's mercy, she gave of herself and built a global "empire of hope." From St. Frances Xavier Cabrini, we can see a witness of love.

2 John 4–9
Psalm 119:1,2,10,11,17,18
Luke 17:26–37

Saturday

NOVEMBER 14

Beloved, you are faithful in all you do for the brothers
and sisters,
especially for strangers;
they have testified to your love before the Church.
Please help them in a way worthy of God
to continue their journey.
—3 JOHN 5–6

Growing up on a farm near a small town far from major highways, I felt excited and amazed every time a visitor showed up. "You mean you traveled all the way here to see this? To be with us?" I marveled. In those days, I learned that hospitality can be shown by offering others kindness, amazement, and curiosity. How could you offer these gifts to others today?

3 John 5–8
Psalm 112:1–2,3–4,5–6
Luke 18:1–8

Sunday

NOVEMBER 15

• THIRTY-THIRD SUNDAY IN ORDINARY TIME •

For all of you are children of the light
and children of the day.
We are not of the night or of darkness.
Therefore, let us not sleep as the rest do,
but let us stay alert and sober.
—1 THESSALONIANS 5:5–6

The Light of the World speaks to you:
I made you to glow, to illumine mercy and truth.
Shine bright, dear one; help others to find their way.
As you shine, you will offer guidance and hope.
With your glow, you may lure others out of darkness.
You are a light, and I love you.

Proverbs 31:10–13,19–20,30–31
Psalm 128:1–2,3,4–5
1 Thessalonians 5:1–6
Matthew 25:14–30

Monday

NOVEMBER 16

• ST. MARGARET OF SCOTLAND * ST. GERTRUDE THE GREAT, VIRGIN •

As Jesus approached Jericho
a blind man was sitting by the roadside begging,
and hearing a crowd going by, he inquired
what was happening.
They told him,
"Jesus of Nazareth is passing by."
—LUKE 18:35–37

Imagine you're there, sitting next to the blind man. You hear stones shuffling and the movement of feet. Voices are animated with joy. The blind man says, "What's happening?" You don't have an answer. You wonder too. Then you overhear someone say, "That's Jesus of Nazareth!" You wonder if he's the savior you're waiting for and that's why people are joyful. Then you exchange glances with Jesus when he passes in front of you. What happens next? What message does Jesus have for you today?

Revelation 1:1–4; 2:1–5
Psalm 1:1–2,3,4 and 6
Luke 18:35–43

Tuesday

NOVEMBER 17

• ST. ELIZABETH OF HUNGARY, RELIGIOUS •

[The Lord said,] "I know your works;
I know that you are neither cold nor hot.
I wish you were either cold or hot.
So, because you are lukewarm, neither hot nor cold,
I will spit you out of my mouth."
—REVELATION 3:15–16

Sometimes, being lukewarm can seem appropriate. Maybe we're afraid that we'll turn people off if we're too enthusiastic. We fear being misunderstood or rejected. We don't want to come off too strong. But the Word of God has harsh words for those times when we don't live our faith wholeheartedly. It is better to be aware of our joys and doubts—to be honest about our level of sincerity—instead of pretending or going through motions. It's better to be hot, not lukewarm.

Revelation 3:1–6,14–22
Psalm 15:2–3a,3bc–4ab,5
Luke 19:1–10

Wednesday

NOVEMBER 18

• THE DEDICATION OF THE BASILICAS OF ST. PETER AND ST. PAUL, APOSTLES
• ST. ROSE PHILIPPINE DUCHESNE, VIRGIN •

[Jesus said,] "His fellow citizens, however, despised him
and sent a delegation after him to announce,
'We do not want this man to be our king.'
But when he returned after obtaining the kingship,
he had the servants called, to whom he had given
the money,
to learn what they had gained by trading."
—LUKE 19:14–15

As a young teacher, I said I was passionate about "empowering youth." I rethought my words, though, when a mentor gently reminded me that the young already had power. No one gives others power; all naturally have power given by God. Yet we are not always conscious of our power to effect change. In today's Gospel, Jesus tells a parable about a man who desired to be king and gave his servants a task to do. The servants stepped into their duty in different ways. Each of us has the freedom to choose how we use our power.

Revelation 4:1–11 or Acts 28:11–16,30–31
Psalm 150:1b–2,3–4,5–6 or 98:1,2–3ab,3cd–4,5–6
Luke 19:11–28 or Matthew 14:22–33

Thursday

NOVEMBER 19

Sing to the LORD a new song
of praise in the assembly of the faithful.
—PSALM 149:1

At the Sacrament of Confirmation, we receive the gifts of the Holy Spirit and become publicly committed Christians. With these graces comes an ability to bear witness, to boldly proclaim how great God is, to share our faith, and to help others know the love and joy of being a Christian. How could you proclaim God's goodness today?

Revelation 5:1–10
Psalm 149:1b–2,3–4,5–6a and 9b
Luke 19:41–44

Friday

NOVEMBER 20

How sweet to my palate are your promises,
sweeter than honey to my mouth!
—PSALM 119:103

Consider your favorite sweets, and how God's covenant is richer. Then offer God a prayer.

God of Love, your ways are sweet and precious. The covenant you made with us long ago is like nectar. Your mercy is like chocolate. Your fidelity and care are refreshing and delicious like ice cream, the kind I am willing to pay a high price for. Today, I long to savor your goodness and delight. Amen.

Revelation 10:8–11
Psalm 119:14,24,72,103,111,131
Luke 19:45–48

Saturday

NOVEMBER 21

• THE PRESENTATION OF THE BLESSED VIRGIN MARY •

When they stood on their feet, great fear fell
on those who saw them.
Then they heard a loud voice from heaven say to them,
"Come up here."
So they went up to heaven in a cloud
as their enemies looked on.
—REVELATION 11:11–12

We believe God is transcendent, above and beyond what we know as ordinary. Yes, God is all powerful, strong, and mighty. God, though, is not out of reach: God is constantly reaching out to us, holding us, and guiding us. God knows the big picture better than we do. So, we surrender to God's power because it instills in us humility and openness. By honoring the power difference between us and God, we accept the reality that we are equal with all humanity. And God is the greatest among us.

Revelation 11:4–12
Psalm 144:1b,2,9–10
Luke 20:27–40

Sunday

NOVEMBER 22

• OUR LORD JESUS CHRIST, KING OF THE UNIVERSE •

The lost I will seek out,
the strayed I will bring back,
the injured I will bind up,
the sick I will heal,
but the sleek and the strong I will destroy,
shepherding them rightly.
—EZEKIEL 34:16

It's the Feast of Christ the King. This is a day to pray about how Christ is the ruler of our hearts, homes, and church. We exalt Jesus because he reigns with gentleness and love. We know him as triumphant because his Incarnation and Resurrection have changed the course of history. We adore him as holy because he serves the weak. With Jesus as King, mercy, justice, equity, and peace are centered in every situation. Christ's kingdom may not dominate in the ways that some would prefer, but we can surrender to the great and transformative love we know in him.

Ezekiel 34:11–12,15–17
Psalm 23:1–2,2–3,5–6 (1)
1 Corinthians 15:20–26,28
Matthew 25:31–46

Monday

NOVEMBER 23

• ST. CLEMENT I, POPE AND MARTYR • ST. COLUMBAN, ABBOT •
BL. MIGUEL AUGUSTÍN PRO, PRIEST AND MARTYR •

[Jesus] said, "I tell you truly,
this poor widow put in more than all the rest;
for those others have all made offerings
from their surplus wealth,
but she, from her poverty, has offered her
whole livelihood."
—LUKE 21:3–4

A grace of being an instrument of God is that we can give and trust that God will provide more than we need. *God of Abundance, I wonder how it could be if I made my offerings from my whole livelihood. How might you need me to stretch out of my comfort zone? I hear so much about conserving my energy and being careful with my resources. Is it possible that you need me to take risks for the sake of others? Guide me, God. And, with your grace, may I say* yes *to bolder generosity. Amen.*

Revelation 14:1–3,4b–5
Psalm 24:1bc–2,3–4ab,5–6
Luke 21:1–4

Tuesday

NOVEMBER 24

• ST. ANDREW DŨNG-LẠC, PRIEST, AND COMPANIONS, MARTYRS •

[Jesus said,] "See that you not be deceived,
for many will come in my name, saying,
'I am he,' and 'The time has come.'
Do not follow them!"
—LUKE 21:8

It seems that we want easy answers and quick resolutions. The reality, though, is that God's ways are mysterious, and God's timing is perfect. Keeping this in mind, we must carefully discern who is attracting our attention and why they tug at our hearts. Why are we tempted to get behind some people and not others? Now is a good time to assess who has captured our hope, and recenter our lives in the truth of Jesus Christ.

Revelation 14:14–19
Psalm 96:10,11–12,13
Luke 21:5–11

Wednesday

NOVEMBER 25

• ST. CATHERINE OF ALEXANDRIA, VIRGIN AND MARTYR •

"Great and wonderful are your works,
Lord God almighty.
Just and true are your ways,
O king of the nations.
Who will not fear you, Lord,
or glorify your name?
For you alone are holy.
All the nations will come
and worship before you,
for your righteous acts have been revealed."
—REVELATION 15:3–4

To this prayer in Revelation, I want to add,
You alone are beauty, truth, and love. You constantly impress me with the magnificent colors and cloud formations moving across the sky. You make me marvel at your designs: from the tiny ants to the enormous elephants, from the cacti to the redwoods. I praise you for your creativity and might. Amen.
Dear reader, what would you add to this prayer?

Revelation 15:1–4
Psalm 98:1,2–3ab,7–8,9
Luke 21:12–19

Thursday

NOVEMBER 26

• THANKSGIVING DAY •

I give thanks to my God always on your account
for the grace of God bestowed on you in Christ Jesus,
that in him you were enriched in every way.
—1 CORINTHIANS 1:4–5

At every celebration of the Eucharist, we are centered in the act of thanksgiving, as the word *Eucharist* means *thanksgiving*. When the bread and wine are offered on the altar and become the body and blood of Jesus Christ, we are being formed in the truth that ought to define our Christian life. Gratitude invites us to share. We are made to be one. Giving thanks is meant to be an ordinary, holy act.

Revelation 18:1–2,21–23; 19:1–3,9a
Psalm 100:1b–2,3,4,5
Luke 21:20–28

PROPER MASS IN THANKSGIVING TO GOD:
Sirach 50:22–24
1 Corinthians 1:3–9
Luke 17:11–19

Friday

NOVEMBER 27

Then I saw a new heaven and a new earth.
The former heaven and the former earth
had passed away,
and the sea was no more.
—REVELATION 21:1

The transformations that are possible with Christ can be dramatic: from militant to pacifist, poverty to wealth, scarcity to abundance, noise to silence, selfishness to service. Discipleship of Jesus Christ is a journey of *metanoia*: a difference in our hearts *and* lives. Let's pray and ponder if we're ready. We're on a path toward drastic, God-directed change.

Revelation 20:1–4,11—21:2
Psalm 84:3,4,5–6a and 8a
Luke 21:29–33

Saturday

NOVEMBER 28

In his hands are the depths of the earth,
and the tops of the mountains are his.
His is the sea, for he has made it,
and the dry land, which his hands have formed.
—PSALM 95:4–5

God's loving hands gently tend to the tiniest creatures deep in the ocean—scallops, coral, and plankton—and the hidden specks of sand along the seashore. On mountaintops, God lovingly claims the newborn mountain goats. The Lord knows the intricate design of every snowflake. And God cares for the wonder of you, your home, your heart, and your needs: every cell is known and beloved, held and cherished. You have an opportunity to respond with praise.

Revelation 22:1–7
Psalm 95:1–2,3–5,6–7ab
Luke 21:34–36

Sunday

NOVEMBER 29

• FIRST SUNDAY OF ADVENT •

Jesus said to his disciples:
"Be watchful! Be alert!
You do not know when the time will come."
—MARK 13:33

Happy First Sunday of Advent—a day to start getting ready for the coming of Christ. Of course, Christ is already present and close, yet the world groans with longing for the fullness of Christ's peace to be known. Sharing Christ's peace is our mission, and this is Advent activity. Where there is war and terror, let us watch for opportunities to teach nonviolence. Where there is captivity and enslavement, let us set people free. Where there is fear and danger, let us respond with compassion and courage and share Christ's love. By our participation, the world will become ready for the coming of the Lord.

Isaiah 63:16b–17,19b; 64:2–7
Psalm 80:2–3,15–16,18–19 (4)
1 Corinthians 1:3–9
Mark 13:33–37

Monday

NOVEMBER 30

• ST. ANDREW, APOSTLE •

As it is written,
How beautiful are the feet of those
who bring the good news!
—ROMANS 10:15

Each day we are sent out to be messengers who share good news. Not to sow judgment, fear, or division, but to bring hope, mercy, and freedom. At offices, in classrooms, or online, we proclaim that others are beloved; they matter, and the church offers them belonging. In ways that are natural to each of us and our circumstances, we share God's love with words, presence, kindness, and service. Today is another day to say *yes* to this joyful mission.

Romans 10:9–18
Psalm 19:8,9,10,11
Matthew 4:18–22

Tuesday

December 1

Not by appearance shall he judge,
nor by hearsay shall he decide,
But he shall judge the poor with justice,
and decide aright for the land's afflicted.
—Isaiah 11:3–4

As we light a candle on the Advent wreath, notice how the flame glimmers brightly and dances through the dark. We conjure up our hopes and questions. We desire justice; we desire to be in right relationship with the land, people, and God. We hope to gain clarity and confidence about the direction of our lives. In the mystery and uncertainty, the darkness can overwhelm. Yet we trust God and believe in the coming of the light.

Isaiah 11:1–10
Psalm 72:1–2,7–8,12–13,17
Luke 10:21–24

Wednesday

DECEMBER 2

Jesus said to them, "How many loaves do you have?"
"Seven," they replied, "and a few fish."
He ordered the crowd to sit down on the ground.
Then he took the seven loaves and the fish,
gave thanks, broke the loaves,
and gave them to the disciples, who in turn
gave them to the crowds.
—MATTHEW 15:34–36

As one of the few stories of Jesus that is told in all four Gospels, this story speaks of abundance. The abundance of graces offered to the crowd that day show us how to be "church." We see how Jesus's beloved people gathered together, offered what they could, prayed with hope and trust, and fed one another. Today, this is how we worship, and this is our mission. We feed when we encourage, help, support, listen, and provide for others' needs. We all give and take, offer and receive. This makes us one. How can you feed others today?

Isaiah 25:6–10a
Psalm 23:1–3a,3b–4,5,6
Matthew 15:29–37

Thursday

DECEMBER 3

• ST. FRANCIS XAVIER, PRIEST •

He humbles those in high places,
and the lofty city he brings down;
He tumbles it to the ground,
levels it with the dust.
It is trampled underfoot by the needy,
by the footsteps of the poor.
—ISAIAH 26:5–6

Biblical justice may seem like a threat to those who have great wealth and privilege. For those who have labored for position and power, it could seem challenging to learn that the Bible promotes downward mobility and humility. With Christ, there is a new meaning of justice than what may seem fair. With God's love as the guide, wealth and power are rearranged. In these Advent days, we each have a part to play in bringing about God's vision for the world. We share, step aside, redistribute, and allow space for justice to arrive.

Isaiah 26:1–6
Psalm 118:1 and 8–9,19–21,25–27a
Matthew 7:21,24–27

Friday

DECEMBER 4

• ST. JOHN DAMASCENE, PRIEST AND DOCTOR OF THE CHURCH •

Wait for the LORD with courage;
be stouthearted, and wait for the LORD.
—PSALM 27:14

During the Advent season, many of us hope for healing. Christ, the healer, is ready to hear our prayers.

Great Physician, I offer you my wounds today. I know I am broken because I am human, because I've been hurt and have endured. I see my scars and feel my aches. I feel my weakness. I need your grace and love. I believe that my brokenness doesn't decrease my dignity or beauty; I know that I am your beloved child. Complete me and heal me, Holy One, so that I am totally yours. Amen.

Isaiah 29:17–24
Psalm 27:1,4,13–14
Matthew 9:27–31

Saturday

DECEMBER 5

The Lord will give you the bread you need and the water for which you thirst.
—ISAIAH 30:20

As we lift another flap on our Advent calendars, we have a chance to check in with God about our longings and hopes. Do we hunger for justice? Are we thirsting for healing? Maybe we simply hope for some more peace and quiet. Let's allow our hopes to bubble to the surface of our contemplation and consider how we're preparing for our prayers to be answered. God provides for all our needs, but we must be open to receiving what's offered.

Isaiah 30:19–21,23–26
Psalm 147:1–2,3–4,5–6
Matthew 9:35—10:1,5a,6–8

Sunday

DECEMBER 6

• SECOND SUNDAY OF ADVENT •

Do not ignore this one fact, beloved,
that with the Lord one day is like a thousand years
and a thousand years like one day.
The Lord does not delay his promise,
as some regard "delay."
—2 PETER 3:8–9

With God, time is more like the lines layered up on the side of a cliff; each moment is apparent and true. Geology reveals great history—stones tell stories about the current moment, and mountains shift toward something new. So too it is with us and our collective relationship with our perfect and provident God. God's timing may be mysterious, but we can trust the steadfastness of grace and mercy. Our impatience and human limitations may erode our hope, but we can surrender to the mystery of God's love.

Isaiah 40:1–5,9–11
Psalm 85:9–10,11–12,13–14 (8)
2 Peter 3:8–14
Mark 1:1–8

Monday

DECEMBER 7

• ST. AMBROSE, BISHOP AND DOCTOR OF THE CHURCH •

The desert and the parched land will exult;
the steppe will rejoice and bloom.
They will bloom with abundant flowers,
and rejoice with joyful song.
—ISAIAH 35:1–2

From deserts to deep seas, each landscape bursts with color, diversity, and potential. In the same way, the landscapes of our lives are made to bloom. As landscapes balance predator and prey, we balance calm and activity in our homes and hearts. As landscapes contain both dying and rising, so too must our faith communities. With Christ, we are not stagnant or stuck. We are made to bloom.

Isaiah 35:1–10
Psalm 85:9ab and 10,11–12,13–14
Luke 5:17–26

Tuesday

DECEMBER 8

• THE IMMACULATE CONCEPTION OF THE BLESSED VIRGIN MARY •

Sing to the LORD a new song,
for he has done wondrous deeds.
—PSALM 98:1

As a girl, I felt embarrassed when I went to church with my grandma. She really loved God and sang loud and off-key. Sometimes she would sing the wrong words or the completely wrong song. Now, as an adult, I often catch myself doing the same thing. I am not embarrassed anymore. It helps to remember what my grandma once said: "The Bible says to make a joyful noise unto the Lord. It doesn't say it has to sound pretty!" On this feast day, let's not be shy. Let's boldly sing out, even if we are off-key.

Genesis 3:9–15,20
Psalm 98:1,2–3ab,3cd–4
Ephesians 1:3–6,11–12
Luke 1:26–38

Wednesday

DECEMBER 9

• ST. JUAN DIEGO CUAUHTLATOATZIN, HERMIT •

Merciful and gracious is the LORD,
slow to anger and abounding in kindness.
Not according to our sins does he deal with us,
nor does he requite us according to our crimes.
—PSALM 103:8 AND 10

I am relieved to know this is who God is: merciful, forgiving, kind, and gracious. If God were operating more like Santa Claus, keeping a list of when I am naughty and nice, then I'd be in big trouble. God would be terrifying instead of a comforting source of all goodness that I trust to hold and help me along. Yet I recognize that many may have the opposite image of God. There are many who are afraid of God's wrath and judgment. How can I help them to know God's love?

Isaiah 40:25–31
Psalm 103:1–2,3–4,8 and 10
Matthew 11:28–30

Thursday

DECEMBER 10

• OUR LADY OF LORETO •

Jesus said to the crowds:
"Amen, I say to you,
among those born of women
there has been none greater than John the Baptist;
yet the least in the Kingdom of heaven
is greater than he."
—MATTHEW 11:11

In the time of Jesus, and now, God sends prophetic voices to help us keep the bigger picture in mind. We must take in the long view and see how our ordinary choices impact generations ahead. The systems and structures we create, the waste we leave behind, the resources we consume—all of it could help or harm. Advent is a good time to tune into these prophetic voices who compel us to reorder our time, resources, and priorities. As we do, we are preparing the way of the Lord.

Isaiah 41:13–20
Psalm 145:1 and 9,10–11,12–13ab
Matthew 11:11–15

Friday

DECEMBER 11

• ST. DAMASUS I, POPE •

[Jesus said,] "The Son of Man came eating and drinking
and they said,
'Look, he is a glutton and a drunkard,
friend of tax collectors and sinners.'
But wisdom is vindicated by her works."
—MATTHEW 11:19

Like those who were critical of Jesus, we may have a particular image of how the Messiah is supposed to be. A lot of us are likely to get behind saviors who seem mighty and powerful, who demonstrate their strength through the use of force. Christ, though, invites us to think outside the box. The Christian way is countercultural and provocative: gentle, humble, joyful, and generous. We give of our time and possessions—we give our very lives—because we believe in a God who changed everything through selflessness. The Incarnation and the Cross show us how to love.

Isaiah 48:17–19
Psalm 1:1–2,3,4 and 6
Matthew 11:16–19

Saturday

DECEMBER 12

• OUR LADY OF GUADALUPE

A great sign appeared in the sky, a woman clothed
with the sun,
with the moon under her feet,
and on her head a crown of twelve stars.
—REVELATION 12:1

Close your eyes and visualize the mother of God. Does Mary look like the vision in Revelation, like Our Lady of Guadalupe, or like your own mother? Maybe she is doing some simple labor, like washing dishes. Or maybe she's sitting on a throne. No matter our culture, time, or place, each of us can be in relationship with the Blessed Mother and come to know her love. Because of God's grace, her power transcends the limits of borders and language.
Mary is for everyone.

Zechariah 2:14–17 or Revelation 11:19a; 12:1–6a,10ab
Judith 13:18bcde,19
Luke 1:26–38 or 1:39–47

Sunday

DECEMBER 13

• THIRD SUNDAY OF ADVENT •

Rejoice always. Pray without ceasing.
In all circumstances give thanks,
for this is the will of God for you in Christ Jesus.
—1 THESSALONIANS 5:16–19

Today is Gaudete Sunday, so we light the rose candle and rejoice. We rejoice because Christ is near, yet Christ is also distant and on his way. This is the glorious "now and not yet," the both/and paradox of heaven and the Kingdom of God. Much like how starlight is currently coming to earth from stars that are lightyears away, we also know Christ as one who both shines through the distant dark *and* illumines what is near. Let us celebrate the beauty and the mystery of God's coming, of Christ's light.

Isaiah 61:1–2a,10–11
Luke 1:46–48,49–50,53–54
1 Thessalonians 5:16–24
John 1:6–8,19–28

Monday

December 14

• ST. JOHN OF THE CROSS, PRIEST AND DOCTOR OF THE CHURCH •

[Balaam said,] "I see him, though not now;
I behold him, though not near:
A star shall advance from Jacob,
and a staff shall rise from Israel."
—NUMBERS 24:17

I've lived with a lot of different people over the years. After I move into a new community, I wait. I wait to notice someone's mannerisms and presence so that I can tell when they are nearby even if I can't see them. And when I sense the arrival of this awareness, I feel more settled and at home. This knowing and beholding of the other who may not be clearly visible to me is much like what happens in prayer. With God and one another, we can feel at home.

Numbers 24:2–7,15–17a
Psalm 25:4–5ab,6 and 7bc,8–9
Matthew 21:23–27

Tuesday

DECEMBER 15

But I will leave as a remnant in your midst
a people humble and lowly,
Who shall take refuge in the name of the LORD:
the remnant of Israel.
—ZEPHANIAH 3:12–13

Like every species made by God, we need to know refuge. Shelter and safety are basic needs, without which we can't rest or flourish. Yet many people are on the move, fleeing danger, oppression, disaster, and poverty. Like Mary and Joseph who had to travel from Nazareth to Bethlehem, and then to Egypt and back to Galilee, travelers are forced to accept discomforts and risks. So how can the name of the Lord offer refuge to all who are in need? Perhaps by the compassion and hospitality offered by the people of God. Let's make room for others today and share our space, food, tables, and homes so others can rest and flourish.

Zephaniah 3:1–2,9–13
Psalm 34:2–3,6–7,17–18,19 and 23
Matthew 21:28–32

Wednesday

DECEMBER 16

Jesus said to them in reply,
"Go and tell John what you have seen and heard:
the blind regain their sight,
the lame walk,
lepers are cleansed,
the deaf hear, the dead are raised,
the poor have the good news proclaimed to them.
And blessed is the one who takes no offense at me."
—LUKE 7:22–23

Doubt is a normal part of being human. There's nothing wrong with being uncertain and asking questions. We don't want to get stuck in that space though. Jesus provides a way forward: we share testimony with one another. We share the Good News and proclaim the truth about the miracles we have witnessed. Each time we do this for others, we can offer clarity, hope, and courage: gifts that matter to the faithful. Let's show others the Light.

Isaiah 45:6c–8,18,21c–25
Psalm 85:9ab and 10,11–12,13–14
Luke 7:18b–23

Thursday

DECEMBER 17

Eleazar became the father of Matthan,
Matthan the father of Jacob,
Jacob the father of Joseph, the husband of Mary.
Of her was born Jesus who is called the Christ.
—MATTHEW 1:15–16

I heard about a man in a remote village who was curious about Christianity and came to a gathering where the genealogy of Jesus from the Gospel of Matthew was read aloud. In that man's culture, if a person was important, they would be introduced along with the names of their parents and grandparents. The more ancestors that were named, the greater the importance of that person. When this man heard the long list of Jesus's ancestors, he was impressed and became a Christian. Jesus remains important today. Let's give him the honor he is due.

Genesis 49:2,8–10
Psalm 72:1–2,3–4ab,7–8,17
Matthew 1:1–17

Friday

DECEMBER 18

Behold, the days are coming, says the LORD,
when I will raise up a righteous shoot to David;
As king he shall reign and govern wisely,
he shall do what is just and right in the land.
—JEREMIAH 23:5

In the northern hemisphere, we are now living in the midst of some of the darkest days of the year. Less daylight impacts our mood, energy, and rhythms. Some may become depressed and tempted to despair. Yet even in the dark, God remains. I love to ponder this by praying beside a lit candle in a dark room. As we wait in the dark for the coming of the Savior, we can savor the sacredness. Let's honor the reality of our feelings and struggles. Let's offer God our hopes.

Jeremiah 23:5–8
Psalm 72:1–2,12–13,18–19
Matthew 1:18–25

Saturday

DECEMBER 19

But the angel said to him, "Do not be afraid, Zechariah,
because your prayer has been heard.
Your wife Elizabeth will bear you a son,
and you shall name him John."
—LUKE 1:13

We prepare for the coming of Christ by gathering together. This time of year, we may go to parties, concerts, and pageants and delight in our joyful tradition. An advantage of being with a community is how it strengthens us. We counter our fears by being in groups and feeling others' energy. We feel inspired when we witness how others bravely stand before us and sing a solo or act out a truth. Like Zechariah learned from the angel, when we are connected to others, we need not be afraid.

Judges 13:2–7,24–25a
Psalm 71:3–4a,5–6ab,16–17
Luke 1:5–25

Sunday

DECEMBER 20

• FOURTH SUNDAY OF ADVENT •

The angel Gabriel was sent from God
to a town of Galilee called Nazareth,
to a virgin betrothed to a man named Joseph,
of the house of David,
and the virgin's name was Mary.
—LUKE 1:26–27

Here we have a testament that reveals how specific and personal God is: sending holy messengers to specific people in a particular time and place. And here you are, in Advent 2026, reading this particular book, praying to the same God that David, Mary, and Joseph each knew and loved. We are special individuals known by God, and we are part of a collective history, a giant human family. As we await the arrival of Christ again, let us ponder how God is present to us through particular people, times, and places, too.

2 Samuel 7:1–5,8b–12,14a,16
Psalm 89:2–3,4–5,27,29 (2a)
Romans 16:25–27
Luke 1:26–38

Monday

DECEMBER 21

• ST. PETER CANISIUS, PRIEST AND DOCTOR OF THE CHURCH •

[Elizabeth said to Mary,] "Most blessed are you among women, and blessed is the fruit of your womb."
—LUKE 1:42

As a woman, I find it meaningful to pray with Mary's pregnancy during the season of Advent. I wonder how her body reacted to the feeling of life within her. I consider how Mary's organs had to shift to make room for the coming of God, how her skin stretched and her body ached with new weight. I talk to Mary about feeling uncomfortable, and I ask her to help me understand how I might stay in a state of grace when I, too, am stretched for the sake of love. No matter who we are, or our state of life, we are each called to accept God's new ways.

Song of Songs 2:8–14 or Zephaniah 3:14–18a
Psalm 33:2–3,11–12,20–21
Luke 1:39–45

Tuesday

DECEMBER 22

[Mary said,] "He has cast down the mighty from their thrones
and has lifted up the lowly.
He has filled the hungry with good things,
and the rich he has sent away empty."
—LUKE 1:52–53

Mary's song—the Magnificat—describes what happens when Love becomes human and the reign of God is established. With Mary's *yes* and Christ's coming, the poor are uplifted and have all their needs met. Equity and justice are abundant. A new order is established. This song is so powerful and revolutionary, and central to our faith, that monks and nuns throughout the globe sing it every evening. And when we feed the hungry, we add harmonious notes to the powerful song. As we act for justice, let's sing with Mary. Come, Lord Jesus.

1 Samuel 1:24–28
1 Samuel 2:1,4–5,6–7,8abcd
Luke 1:46–56

Wednesday

DECEMBER 23

• ST. JOHN OF KANTY, PRIEST •

He guides the humble to justice,
he teaches the humble his way.
—PSALM 25:9

For Christians, humility is a grace—a grace we can pray for. *Humble me, O Lord. Help me to know the truth of who I am and how I belong to you. Help me to set aside what is false and the temptation to make myself great. I may want to be something I am not and might be trying too hard to become something untrue. I need you, God of truth, to teach me who I really am. Show me how to surrender to your will and your way. I love you, and I belong to you. Amen.*

Malachi 3:1–4,23–24
Psalm 25:4–5ab,8–9,10 and 14
Luke 1:57–66

Thursday

DECEMBER 24

[Zechariah prophesied,] "He has raised up for us a mighty Savior,
born of the house of his servant David.
Through his prophets he promised of old
that he would save us from our enemies,
from the hands of all who hate us.
He promised to show mercy to our fathers
and to remember his holy covenant."

—LUKE 1:69–72

On this night, Christmas Eve, we are graced with an opportunity to consider how our story fits with all of salvation history. When we gather in church with our neighbors and family, we can remember how we are part of a covenant people whom God has faithfully protected and guided for centuries. We rejoice and give praise for the goodness of God's love, a love that connects us to a lineage and pours out into the future. This love has come to be with us: a vulnerable infant born in humility. This love story changes everything, in the best of ways.

2 Samuel 7:1–5,8b–12,14a,16
Psalm 89:2–3,4–5,27 and 29
Luke 1:67–79

Friday

DECEMBER 25

• THE NATIVITY OF THE LORD (CHRISTMAS) •

Now there were shepherds in that region
living in the fields
and keeping the night watch over their flock.
The angel of the Lord appeared to them
and the glory of the Lord shone around them,
and they were struck with great fear.
—LUKE 2:8–9

In first-century Palestine, shepherds had little privilege, status, or wealth, and yet these are the people to whom God announced his arrival. As we meditate on the transformative power of Love taking on human flesh, we praise God for the love that continues to upset the status quo and celebrate by declaring justice and peace to the poor and the least among us.

VIGIL:
Isaiah 62:1–5
Psalm 89:4–5,16–17,27,29 (2a)
Acts 13:16–17,22–25
Matthew 1:1–25

NIGHT:
Isaiah 9:1–6
Psalm 96:1–2,2–3,11–12,13
Titus 2:11–14
Luke 2:1–14

DAWN:
Isaiah 62:11–12
Psalm 97:1,6,11–12
Titus 3:4–7
Luke 2:15–20

DAY:
Isaiah 52:7–10
Psalm 98:1,2–3,3–4,5–6 (3c)
Hebrews 1:1–6
John 1:1–18

Saturday

DECEMBER 26

• ST. STEPHEN, THE FIRST MARTYR •

Jesus said to his disciples:
"Beware of men, for they will hand you over to courts
and scourge you in their synagogues,
and you will be led before governors and kings
for my sake
as a witness before them and the pagans."
—MATTHEW 10:17–18

It's the day after Christmas, and many of us may want to remain festive. The last thing we may be in the mood for is celebrating the feast of a martyr, reflecting on the actual cost of discipleship. After all, Christmas cookies are much sweeter than praying with the suffering. Yet the reality is that Christmas isn't an easy time for everyone. Many feel the absence of their loved ones. Others are aware of their disappointments and grief. Today could be a good day to reach out to someone who is struggling and hold their heaviness in prayer.

Acts 6:8–10; 7:54–59
Psalm 31:3cd–4,6 and 8ab,16bc and 17
Matthew 10:17–22

Sunday

DECEMBER 27

• THE HOLY FAMILY OF JESUS, MARY, AND JOSEPH •

The Lord took Abram outside and said,
"Look up at the sky and count the stars, if you can.
Just so," he added, "shall your descendants be."
Abram put his faith in the LORD,
who credited it to him as an act of righteousness.
—GENESIS 15:5–6

This story cracks me up. Although the poetic narrative makes it sound like it was a serious moment shared by God and Abram, I can imagine God teasingly asking Abram to count the stars, knowing it was impossible. And I can imagine Abram bursting into laughter as he became filled with freedom and joy, grateful for God's care. In the same way, in our families and in the Holy Family, caring conversations can fill us with freedom and joy.

Genesis 15:1–6; 21:1–3 or Sirach 3:2–6,12–14
Psalm 105:1–2,3–4,5–6,8–9 (7a, 8a)
Hebrews 11:8,11–12,17–19 or Colossians 3:12–21
Luke 2:22–40

Monday

DECEMBER 28

• THE HOLY INNOCENTS, MARTYRS •

When Herod realized that he had been deceived
by the magi,
he became furious.
He ordered the massacre of all the boys in Bethlehem
and its vicinity
two years old and under.
—MATTHEW 2:16

We know the horror continues: infants die in poverty, children are victims of violence, and the unborn don't get to be born. We may squirm at the statement that we're celebrating a feast today. Yet if we ignore the darkness of the story of Christmas—the horrors countered by the redemptive love of the Incarnation—then we could be blinded by the light of Christ's life. Let's lament and pray with the heartache. Let's invite Christ's love to heal us.

1 John 1:5—2:2
Psalm 124:2–3,4–5,7b–8
Matthew 2:13–18

Tuesday

DECEMBER 29

• ST. THOMAS BECKET, BISHOP AND MARTYR •

This is the way we may know that we are
in union with him:
whoever claims to abide in him ought to walk just
as he walked.
—1 JOHN 2:5–6

Christ speaks to you:
My dear friend, I see you. I see how you pick up this book and hold it, read the word, and enter into your heart space. You're doing so much to care for those in need. You are involved, generous, and kind. This is good, and it all means so much to me. And I am hoping, dear one, that you also see me. See how I walk with you. Notice my movements and moods. I am playful and gentle. I am the Way. You can trust and follow me.

1 John 2:3–11
Psalm 96:1–2a,2b–3,5b–6
Luke 2:22–35

Wednesday

DECEMBER 30

There was a prophetess, Anna,
the daughter of Phanuel, of the tribe of Asher.
She was advanced in years,
having lived seven years with her husband after
her marriage,
and then as a widow until she was eighty-four.
She never left the temple,
but worshiped night and day with fasting and prayer.
And coming forward at that very time,
she gave thanks to God and spoke about the child
to all who were awaiting the redemption
of Jerusalem.
—LUKE 2:36–38

Praying with Anna, we see hope and devotion. Looking at her life, we are inspired to stay steadfast and trust in the mystery of God's Providence. How else does Anna's witness influence your faith journey?

1 John 2:12–17
Psalm 96:7–8a,8b–9,10
Luke 2:36–40

Thursday

DECEMBER 31

• ST. SYLVESTER I, POPE •

Thus we know this is the last hour.
—1 JOHN 2:18

In the early years of Christianity, the faithful were alert. Jesus said that he's coming back, so we must be ready, they figured. For centuries, this openness and receptivity to what may be surprising and transformative has defined Christian discipleship. As the year 2026 winds down, let us give our souls a chance to notice when we have been alert and open to God's surprising ways, and when we could have been more compassionate or merciful. Let's express our thanksgiving, sorrow, and praise. Let us get ready to receive the goodness of God's grace in the year to come.

1 John 2:18–21
Psalm 96:1–2,11–12,13
John 1:1–18